YOU CAN BEAT CITY HALL

YOU CAN BEAT
CITY HALL

W. Bernard Richland

RAWSON, WADE PUBLISHERS, INC.

New York

Library of Congress Cataloging in Publication Data

Richland, W Bernard.
  You can beat city hall.

  Includes index.
  1. Municipal corporations—United States.
  2. Liability (law)—United States.   I.   Title.
KF1302.A2R49   342.73′088   79–67640
ISBN 0–89256–125–4
LC: 79–67640

Published simultaneously in Canada by McClelland and
    Stewart, Ltd.
Manufactured in the United States of America
Composition by American–Stratford Graphic Services,
    Brattleboro, Vermont
Printed and bound by R. R. Donnelley & Sons, Co.
    Crawfordsville, Indiana
Designed by Jacques Chazaud
First Edition

To
Pauline

and

Robin
Lisa
Seth
Alexandra
Rafael

CONTENTS

YOU CAN BEAT CITY HALL

INTRODUCTION

Changing Sides

Local government dominates our lives. Federal and state governments, for the most part, only hand down policy; it is on the city, county, town, and village level that the actual ordering of society—its preservation, its protection, its serving—takes place. More than eighteen years of my professional life has been devoted to acting as lawyer to municipal government; fifteen years as an Assistant Corporation Counsel and three years as Corporation Counsel of New York City. And New York City is, by far, the largest single collection of local government agencies in the nation. When my term of office ended, I decided to see how the other side looked. I was appointed Adjunct Professor of Local Government Law at New York Law School and introduced a course officially titled Local Government Law and Practice. It was actually a series of fourteen lectures for final year law students on how a young lawyer can make a living suing the city.

There is nothing like changing sides to give an advocate a brand new perspective. *Them* becomes *us,* and *us* becomes *them.* The complex of statutes designed to protect municipalities against false claims becomes a mine field across which a careful path must be drawn. The special procedural rules for actions against local governments become traps for unwary citizens. Dedicated public servants become bureaucrats who must be frustrated in the interest of justice. Lapses from rectitude by officials loom as corruption to be ferreted out and corrected. Shortcuts in contracting that favor the *ins* are skullduggery to the *outs*. The tax collector bent upon getting the very last penny of revenue is viewed as a cold-eyed bounty hunter by the taxpayer. Such a new viewpoint creates a different attitude. And from this new perspective, this book has been developed. It opens up the mystique of local governments to the common man, explaining how and when to sue municipalities and how to cope with them effectively.

CHAPTER I

Sueable Cities

What's in a Name?

OUR SYSTEM (if it can be so-called) of local government is the product of our history and the American talent for adapting and modifying existing forms, inventing new ones, and changing them to meet changing circumstances. We are a nation now grown to fifty states. Each state, before it became one, was a collection of local units that sprang up and developed expressly in response to the needs and conditions of the times. Unlike those of the European nations, our local governments are not uniform in structure, nor do they conform to a fixed pattern. Even their titles are varied—counties, parishes, towns, townships, boroughs, and villages.

The basic form of local government in the older states, New England for example, is the county. There are sixty-two counties in New York alone. But the same nomenclature has been copied in other states, and there are about 3,000 counties in the nation. New England has approximately 1,400 towns. There are towns and townships in Michigan, New York, New Jersey, Pennsylvania, and Wisconsin that have significant functions, but most of the country's 15,700 towns are primarily rural. But we are not finished. There are, of course, the cities themselves, which vary in population from 1,200 in Sherrill, New York to 7,800,000 in New York City which embraces five counties. To confuse matters further, each of New York City's five counties is also a borough. Finally, there are the villages, numbering in the thousands throughout the country, some formally organized and some not.

There is only one sure thing about all this: you can no more tell the nature of something called a city, county, town, parish, or village in our great land than you can tell a book by its cover.

This fact makes it difficult to know who to sue in a given situation. But that problem is more apparent than real. Where and to whom you make your claim depends upon what unit of local government is responsible for injuring you or your property, taking your property unlawfully, overtaxing you, or oppressing you. In general, localities mark their property proudly with their insignia. Whether it is a county hospital, a city cemetery, a village park, or a town sewer system, the name of the mayor, the county supervisor, or the village trustee is plastered all over the facility. And it is easy enough to tell if a pot-holed road is a village street or a town or a county road.

But if there is a question, a simple check at the village or city hall will provide simple answers that can be confirmed by looking at official maps and documents. It is not really very difficult. Just ask, check, and ask again.

Types of Suits

There are more than 38,000 cities, counties, parishes, towns, and villages in the United States, and more than 25,000 other local governmental entities, such as independent school and special districts, boards, and other municipal authorities. All of them commit a variety of *torts*, or wrongful acts that inflict physical damage. These are distinguished, for example, from contract violations and suits to compel city officials to obey the law. That is what *tort* meant in Norman French, and lawyers are still addicted to the term more than 900 years after the Battle of Hastings. These local government entities have:

- Cars and trucks that run people down
- Machines that maim
- Pot-holed roads
- Sidewalks that collapse
- Unsafe parks
- Unsupervised playgrounds and schoolyards
- Unguarded swimming pools
- Sewers that overflow
- Open manholes
- Watermains that break
- Safety inspectors who fail to inspect
- Cops who shoot the victim instead of the thief

This list is typical of the kinds of injuries that make up the municipal catalogue of torts. Of course, to the extent that they operate different kinds of facilities and institutions, local governments become liable for other torts. For example, if a city operates a hospital, its physicians, nurses, and staff can injure people by medical malpractice. If it runs a cemetery, it might bulldoze a gravestone. If it operates a housing project, a city can commit every kind of tort that any landlord might from defective elevators and slippery floors to fires caused by negligence. Municipal airports generate their own torts, and so do city transit systems, libraries, and community television aerials.

Local governments injure people in other ways as well.

- They can and often do overtax.
- They can and often do oppress, badger, bully, and impose upon people.
- They can and often do favor the powerful and take advantage of the powerless.

• They can and often do permit unpleasant trades in residential neighborhoods.

And cities, like people and corporations, break their promises, violate contracts, break leases, create ugly nuisances, pollute the air, befoul rivers and streams, and commit other disagreeable acts which result in lawsuits, claims, and screams of outrage.

For all these reasons cities, towns, counties, villages, and other forms of local government are the most sued and the most sueable of all entities. And because they are so sueable, they have been provided with a variety of legal traps and limitations. These traps can be avoided and these limitations can be overcome—if you know how. And, in most cases, it won't cost you a thin dime.

A Bit of History

The technical term for local government is municipal corporation. It was to such corporations that William Hone referred in his nineteenth-century work, *The Table Book:*

> Mr. Howel Walsh, in a corporation case tried in Tralee assizes, observed that "a corporation cannot blush. It was a body, it was true; had certainly a head—a new one every year—an annual acquisition of intelligence in every new lord mayor. Arms, he supposed it had, and very long ones too, for it could reach at anything. Legs, of course, when it made such long strides. A throat to swallow the rights of the community and a stomach to digest them. But whoever yet discovered in the anatomy of any corporation, either bowels or a heart?"

Apparently, the *corporation* did not have a good name among the Irish of Tralee. Nor among the English. It took the Corporation Act of 1661 to bring municipal officers into line, compelling them to "acknowledge the supremacy of the King," to "accept the doctrine of passive obedience," and to "abjure Presbyterianism." Passive obedience is hardly the style of municipal officials today, and the abjuration of Presbyterianism is not a serious problem in our major municipalities. The supremacy of the King of England was only briefly a concern of the City of Chicago during Mayor Thompson's[1] regime in the twenties and no longer bothers any of our municipalities. But the general attitude of the municipal officials reflected in the Tralee assizes and the Corporation Act of 1661 has not changed radically. The local bureaucrat is still viewed as the implacable and arrogant wielder of mysterious power.

Know Your Rights

You have to know that you have rights before you can assert them. And once you know what your rights are, you have to know how to protect them.

In 1978 the think tank of the Rand Corporation, under a National Institute of Health grant, produced a study on medical malpractices that showed—contrary to the popular notion that physicians are sadly put upon by grasping negligence lawyers—that only a minor fraction of all serious reported incidents of medical malpractice resulted in claims against the responsible physicians and hospitals. The same can be said about damages and injuries inflicted on people by municipal governments. Either out of timidity or ignorance people simply do not know or do not assert their rights or neglect to assert them in time. Perhaps the phenomenon is a vestige of the ancient doctrine of *sovereign immunity,* buried deep in the unconscious of a society that fears and respects govern-

---

1. He achieved fame when he promised that in the unlikely event that George V showed up in Chicago, he would "punch him in the nose."

ment. The great majority of victims of municipal government mischief or misconduct accept their injuries as their lot in life. Governments, they feel, are all-powerful, and suing is an expensive business.

Each immigrant group voiced its frustration in its own way. From the Irish we get the expression "Go sue City Hall," the utterly hopeless task for those afflicted by a malign fate. The Jews, seeking out ultimate origins for the slings and arrows of outrageous municipal oppression, typically exclaimed, "A cholera on Columbus." The most resigned is the Italian "Baccigalup," which needs a special explanation. It is all that has survived of the original, "What's the use, in the end Baccigalupo will get you." Baccigalupo was the popular Italian undertaker of immigrant days.

Actually, cities, counties, and towns are generally highly sueable. And lawyers, knowing that cities are good for the money, will represent claimants in accident cases for a contingency fee—that is a fee measured by the amount recovered. This subject will be covered in more detail later.

The Torts of Kings

The notion of *sovereign immunity* is one of the strangest of the law's many curious aspects and customs. It simply means that a state, being a sovereign entity, can be sued only when and if it chooses to be sued. It is a rule that was once universally accepted in all states and, as we shall see, is now applicable in a limited degree to municipalities. It is still in effect in several municipalities, partly so in others, and gradually dying out. The courts, which dearly love the ancient and arcane, trace this doctrine to the English common law maxim, "The King can do no wrong." This is not to say that the king is incapable of anything but virtue, but that since the subject lives by the king's will, whatever the king does is perfectly all right as far as the king is concerned and therefore simply cannot be wrong, no matter how it seems to the victim. This curious idea was adopted by our courts early, despite the fact that our nation owes its very existence to the "wrongdoing" of George III. More curious still, is the fact that it was long ago abandoned in England, from whence it came.

The importance of the rule of sovereign immunity is that it was early extended to municipalities to exempt them from liability for injuries and damages inflicted in the course of their exercise of sovereign or "governmental"—as distinguished from "proprietary"—functions and powers. An explanation is in order. Keeping order and putting out fires are normal governmental activities. But selling water, gas and electricity, or collecting garbage are proprietary activities, commonly conducted by private business. So, says the sovereign immunity rule, if local police and fire personnel cause damage to persons and property in the course of policing or firefighting, their municipal employer cannot be called to account even if their employees are at fault.

What is governmental and what is proprietary for municipal damage action purposes is a great puzzle. Generations of judges and scholars have struggled with the question. Some states have given up on it altogether, and by court decision[2] (as in New York, for example), or legislation, decided that the government is liable to suit for anything a private person would be.

---

2. This came about in a funny way. A five-year-old gelding named Clipper—"moderate type, neither keen nor dull, with no runaway tendencies"—threw his New York City mountie, Patrolman Harry Fagan, and was off and running, as the city's lawyer noted in his brief, "observing all traffic signals and proceeding at a moderate pace." A hero cabbie, Ed Bernadino, tried to stop the horse and was knocked down and injured. He sued the city, which defended on the ground that it was immune from suit for injuries arising out of police activities other than those caused by police vehicles, which Clipper was not. The court held that the city had no sovereign immunity, and the hero cabbie won a judgment of $12,000.

So, if you must be run over by a municipal vehicle in a city that adheres to the sovereign immunity concept, choose a garbage truck, not a fire engine. And if you must pick a fire engine, it might be better to choose one coming *from* a fire (as an Ohio court once decided) rather than one going *to* a fire; or better still, select one on its way to pick up a six-pack for the battalion chief.

Even states that have modified or abandoned the doctrine of sovereign immunity for the torts of municipalities have done so grudgingly, fixing dollar limits on the extent to which municipalities can be held liable. Those limits range from $10,000 for injury to one person in an accident and $20,000 for all injuries arising out of a single occurrence in Kentucky to $30,000 and $5,000,000 in Indiana, with a mean of $100,-000–$300,000 in nineteen other states. Several states have $20,000, $25,000 and $50,000 limits. Strangely, Wisconsin, a state with a liberal tradition, limits municipal liability in accident cases to $25,000.

The best place to have a municipal government accident is in New York City, which pays out more than $30 million each year for tort claims and has set no legal limits on claims for its citizens and visitors. The worst place to have an accident is Arkansas, which has close to total municipal immunity. Maryland is almost as bad. A tabulation of limits on municipal liability follows.

Limits on Municipal Liability

Alabama: No general immunity, but the maximum amount of recovery is fixed at $100,000 per claim and $300,000 per accident, regardless of how many claims.

Alaska: Total immunity is claimed from liability for injuries resulting from failure to inspect or to prevent law violations; licensing; emergency public safety activities and fire department.

Arizona: Immunity generally covers governmental activities; none for nongovernmental activities.

Arkansas: Total governmental immunity, except that municipalities are required to carry auto liability insurance to the same extent as private parties.

California: Governmental immunity has been waived. Liability has been imposed except for discretionary, licensing and inspection activities, the issuance or non-issuance of permits, and misrepresentation of officers or employees.

Colorado: Liability is limited to injuries in motor vehicle accidents, in hospitals, in jails, on streets and sidewalks, in public buildings, and by publicly owned utilities. Damages are limited to $100,000 per person and $300,000 per accident, regardless of number of persons involved. Government employees have limited indemnification, but police have broad indemnification.

Connecticut: Governmental activities are immune. Employees are generally indemnified for civil rights violations.

Delaware: Immunity is claimed for governmental activities, but not for proprietary activities.

Florida: Liability is limited to $50,000 per injury claim and $100,000 per accident, regardless of number of claims.

Georgia: General immunity is claimed, except for injuries from known street defects or municipally created "nuisance."

Hawaii: Immunity pertains only to injuries caused by discretionary acts, enforcement of laws (whether valid or invalid), and collection of taxes.

Idaho: There is no immunity except for injuries from discretionary functions, enforcement of laws, riots and civil disturbances, and road and street design. The limits of recovery are $100,000 per person; $300,000 per accident regardless of number of persons; and $100,000 for property damage.

Illinois: No immunity exists except for injuries in parks and recreation facilities, discretionary acts, inspection failure, and lack of police service. Police are indemnified in cities of over 500,000.

Indiana: There is no liability for injuries from discretionary, judicial, legislative, or licensing acts, inspection failure, law enforcement (but liable for false imprisonment), and natural and temporary street or reservoir conditions resulting from weather. Also, the government is not liable for unintentional misrepresentation. The limits on recovery are $300,000 per person, and $5 million per accident.

Iowa: The government is liable, except for injuries from discretionary acts, legislative functions, law enforcement with due care, and tax collection.

Kansas: The government is generally immune, but is liable for municipal nuisance, and street defects.

Kentucky: There is no liability for injuries from governmental activities. Limits on recovery for motor vehicle accidents are $10,000 per person; $20,000 per accident, regardless of number of persons involved; and $5,000 for property damage.

Louisiana: Immunity has been waived.

Maine: Governmental immunity is claimed except for motor vehicles and equipment, utilities, and public buildings.

Maryland: Governmental immunity is claimed; there is no immunity for proprietary functions.

Massachusetts: The government agreed to limited waivers after the courts threatened total abolition of immunity. Exemption still exists for acts or omissions in carrying out a statute, municipal ordinance or regulation (whether or not valid), intentional assault, false imprisonment, false arrest, malicious prosecution, libel and slander, deceit, invasion of privacy, or any claim arising out of assessment or collection of taxes or the detention of goods by a law enforcement officer.

Michigan: Immunity is claimed for governmental activities. Municipalities are liable for accidents arising out of street and highway defects, accidents in public buildings and on public property, and accidents involving municipal motor vehicles.

Minnesota: No immunity is claimed except for snow and ice on streets, discretionary and legislative acts, and enforcement of law with due care. Limits on claims are $25,000 for death; $50,000 for other accidents; and $300,000 per occurrence regardless of how many people involved. The municipal vehicle limit is $30,000 per injury.

Mississippi: No liability is claimed for governmental activities; liability for proprietary activities is limited to amount of insurance coverage.

Missouri: Liability for governmental activities is limited to amount of insurance carried.

Montana: Governmental immunity was abolished by state constitution, except as provided by the legislature. Municipal liability exists to the extent of insurance purchased. This excludes liability for legislative acts and enforcement of laws. Liability is limited to $300,000 per claim and $1 million per occurrence regardless of the number of claimants.

Nebraska: The government is liable except for injuries arising out of discretionary functions, enforcement of laws, assessments and collection of taxes, quarantines, and road and street defects. Liability is limited to amount of insurance coverage.

Nevada: General liability exists except for injuries from discretionary, legislative, inspection functions, and enforcement of laws. The maximum recovery is $25,000.

New Hampshire: Indemnification is provided for all municipal employees in actions under federal civil rights laws. Governmental immunity was abrogated by the courts and reinstated by statute. Liability is limited to the extent of insurance coverage.

New Jersey: There is general liability for governmental activities except for injuries arising out of discretionary, legislative, judicial, licensing and inspection functions, and the enforcement of law in good faith.

New Mexico: General immunity exists except for injuries from motor vehicles, from aircraft, in public buildings and parks, from machinery and equipment, in airports, from utilities operations (other than failure to provide service), in medical and health facilities, on streets and highways, and from false arrest. Limits on liability are $100,000 for property damage and $300,000 for other claims. Municipalities are required to defend and indemnify employees.

New York: Immunity has been waived except in suits or actions involving legislative, judicial, and prosecutorial functions. Municipal officers and employees are required to be indemnified for violations of federal civil rights laws.

North Carolina: General immunity exists for governmental activities. Municipalities may waive immunity to the extent of insurance coverage.

North Dakota: The government is generally liable, but limits are set at $20,000 per person and $100,000 per occurrence, regardless of number of persons involved.

Ohio: The municipality is immune while carrying out governmental activities, but is liable for proprietary activities. Immune activities are covered to extent of liability insurance.

Oklahoma: General liability exists except immunity for injuries arising out of discretionary activities, licensing, inspection, taxes, law enforcement, temporary conditions, and nuisances. Municipalities are required to indemnify and defend officers and employees.

Oregon: General liability exists with immunity only for discretionary, legislative, and judicial functions, for assessment and collection of taxes, riots and civil disturbances, and for enforcement of laws in good faith. Liability limits are $50,000 for an individual; and $100,000 per occurrence, regardless of number of individuals involved.

Pennsylvania: Sovereign immunity was abrogated by judicial decision in 1973.

Rhode Island: Municipalities are liable for injuries in governmental activities to a maximum of $50,000. There is no limit to monetary recovery for injuries arising from proprietary activities.

South Carolina: The government is immune. Municipalities are liable for street defects and motor vehicle accidents, but liability is limited to $150,000 per person, $300,000 per accident regardless of number of persons involved. There is a $100,000 limit in property damage cases.

South Dakota: Governmental immunity is claimed. Insurance to cover municipal officers and employees is authorized but not required.

Tennessee: The municipality is responsible for motor vehicles, streets and highways, and public structures. Limits are set at $20,000 per person, $40,000 per accident regardless of number of persons involved. However, in the case of a motor vehicle accident, limits are set at $50,000 for property damage and personal injury to one claimant, and $300,000 per accident regardless of number of persons involved.

Texas: There is unlimited liability for accidents arising from proprietary functions. Limits on accidents from governmental functions for negligent operation of motor vehicles and equipment are $100,000 per person, $300,000 for two or more persons, and $10,000 for property damage.

Utah: Immunity is claimed for governmental functions. Governmental immunity is waived to the extent of insurance carried.

Vermont: Governmental immunity is claimed by municipalities, except to the extent that they carry insurance.

Virginia: Governmental immunity is claimed.

Washington: The municipality is liable to the same extent as private persons.

West Virginia: Municipal immunity is waived only to the extent of insurance carried.

Wisconsin: The government is generally liable for torts, but the recovery limit is set at $25,000.

Wyoming: Governmental immunity has been abolished to the extent of insurance carried.

Choosing a Lawyer

In general, it is advisable to retain an attorney to handle the more complex municipal suits, and I will indicate the need for legal assistance in the appropriate chapters. Of course, before you can even think about getting a lawyer, you must be aware of the fact that there is an occasion for doing so; in short, you should be certain that suit can be brought or other legal action taken. That means you must know what your rights are, and that is the main concern of this book.

The selection of a proper attorney can be vital to the success of your claim and the protection of your rights. There are special areas of municipal law that require special knowledge. A good general practice lawyer—like the internist in medicine—will usually know which lawyers in your community are specialists in the area of municipal government law and practice that is applicable to your case—negligence, malpractice, zoning and variances, contracts, licenses and permits, tax assessment proceedings, condemnation, and others. Generally, municipal government specialists cover several areas. The leading legal directory is the multi-volume Martindale-Hubbell, which lists principal law firms and their specialties, particularly for the large cities. Martindale-Hubbell is available in reference libraries. There are also various law lists with more limited coverage, which are usually found in law offices. Local bar associations and the trial lawyers associations (state and national) also offer information on this subject. Since the Supreme Court has now prohibited the long practiced ban upon legal advertising, newspapers, radio, and television carry such advertisements. My preference is still the established lawyers directories and bar association sources of advice. Make a phone call to the local bar association. It will supply you with the names of several lawyers. Do not hesitate to talk with each of the recommended lawyers and make an independent choice.

As noted in later chapters, there are certain types of municipal litigation that lend themselves to the contingent fee method. This is an arrangement in which the lawyer agrees to work for a share of what he recovers for the client. This method is particularly applicable in negligence, malpractice, tax assessment proceedings, and condemnation matters. The usual contingency fee percentage for these different classes of suits will be indicated in the appropriate chapters.

If at any time you are dissatisfied with the lawyer you have retained, you need not continue your relationship. Regardless of whether you have a signed retainer, you are always free to change your attorney. Lawyers understand this and are generally willing to supersede other lawyers. And if a contingency fee arrangement has been made, it is commonly carried over, with the lawyers sharing the fee on the basis of the work performed by each.

If you sue a local government that is not your own, it is generally best to use a local lawyer who is more likely to know local rules and local people. Or pick a lawyer like one I know who, in addressing a small-town jury on behalf of his client, told of a callow youth from that town who moved to the big city after his parents' death, struggled through law school, worked hard, and by true grit and guts succeeded in his profession and returned to prove his mettle before his home town folks. After he got a jury verdict, his client expressed surprise that the lawyer had not mentioned that he came from the town where the trial was held. "I didn't," said the lawyer. "And if you (and the jury) had listened more carefully, you would have noticed that I didn't say I was the fellow I was talking about."

An intelligent non-lawyer can deal with certain municipal problems: the initial stages of seeking a zoning variance, for example; negotiations on licensing; some initial aspects of tax assessment disagreements; even, to a limited extent, in condemnation proceedings, which permit the government to take your property. But, and it is a big *BUT,* do not try to litigate anything but a small claim by yourself, and only then in a small claims court set up to deal with non-lawyer situations. In contingent fee situations, however, you are far better off and in a much less risky position.

CHAPTER II

The Notice Trap

The Notice of Claim Gambit

It is an almost uniform rule in all states that in order to sue a municipality in an accident case, or since you are now better educated, a tort case, a written notice of claim must first be served on the municipality, usually within a short time after the accident occurs. Furthermore, suit on that claim must be brought promptly—sometimes within one year. In theory, this is done because municipalities are usually large and complex organizations, and unless they get prompt notice of impending suits they will be at a serious disadvantage and their taxpayers will suffer. Actually, notice of claim laws serve to reduce the number of suits against municipal governments since a significant percentage of injured persons are not aware of the requirement. Thus, their claims are defeated before suit can be brought into court.

Tort notice of claim requirements are varied and often technical, requiring detailed and specific information. Almost all of them are unreasonable. Some require service of a notice within ten days after the accident, others thirty days, sixty days, or ninety days; there are even some that require service within three days. Here is a list of some of the various municipal tort notice of claim statutes and their time requirements. It is not complete because some of the requirements are hidden away in city, town, county, and village ordinances in places known only to local lawyers specializing in such matters and uncommunicative municipal clerks. (There are other notice of claim laws for contract and other commercial claims against municipalities; they will be discussed later.)

Notice of Claim Requirements

Alabama: Six months after accident; 90 days from injury in Birmingham.

California: 100 days after accident.

Colorado: 90 days after discovery of injury.

Connecticut: City or borough, 30 days after injury from mob; town, city or borough, six months after accident.

District of Columbia: Six months after injury or damage sustained.

Georgia: Six months after actual event.

Idaho: 120 days from date claim arose or injury was discovered, whichever is later.

Illinois: One year from date of injury.

Indiana: 180 days after loss occurred.

Iowa: Commence action within six months unless notice presented within 60 days.

Kansas: Six months after injury.

Kentucky: 90 days after occurrence from defect in thoroughfare.

Maine: 14 days after injury or damage from defective highway, town road, causeway, or bridge.

Maryland: 180 days after injury or damage sustained.

Massachusetts: 30 days after injury from defective road, but failure to give such notice is no defense in snow or ice cases unless the municipality can prove that it was harmed by such failure.

Michigan: 180 days after injury.

Minnesota: 60 days after loss or injury discovered, but none for intentional tort or accident involving motor vehicle.

Missouri: All notice of claim requirements concern street defects. Cities of first class, 60 days; of second class, 30 days; of third class, 90 days; of fourth class, 90 days; of 100,000 inhabitants, 90 days. (Class depends on population.)

Montana: 120 days from date claim arose or imputed discovery, whichever is earlier.

Nevada: Six months from accident.

New Hampshire: 60 days before commencement of action, except 10 days from date of injury on bridge, culvert, or embankment.

New Jersey: 90 days after accident.

New York: 90 days after accident.

North Dakota: 90 days after injury.

Oklahoma: For other than death, 30 days after loss or injury; for death, one year after injury.

Oregon: For other than death, 180 days after loss or injury; for death, one year after injury.

Pennsylvania: Six months from accident; for metropolitan transportation authority, six months after accident.

Rhode Island: 60 days from injury on highway or bridge.

South Carolina: Three months from injury.

South Dakota: 60 days after injury.

Tennessee: 90 days after injury for street and highway defects.

Texas: Except where there is actual notice, six months from date of incident.

Utah: Against city or incorporated town, six months after injury or damage. Against any other political subdivision, 90 days after accident.

Vermont: For bridge or culvert, 20 days after occurrence.

Virginia: Six months after accident.

Washington: 120 days after accident, or 120 days after date damage sustained.

Wisconsin: Town and county liability for highway defects, 120 days after the event. For all other tort actions same period, but noncompliance with notice requirements is no bar if defendant has *actual* notice and the injured party can show that the municipality was not harmed by lack of formal notice.

Wyoming: City or town liability for bridge, street, sidewalk, or thoroughfare defects, 30 days after injury or damage.

The accident lawyer's nightmare usually revolves around notice of claim mishaps: filed one day late; filed at the wrong window in the right place; the right window in the wrong place; with the wrong official; misidentified vehicle; misidentified location; or the wrong time of day. The list of horrible examples is almost endless. Some typical examples follow, not to make your blood run cold, but as a warning of what might happen to you.

At noon on January 4, Mrs. J. returned to her nice, neat little house in Winston-Salem after shopping to find the entire ground floor of her house a foot deep in raw sewage—living room, dining room, den, and kitchen. A city road grader team had flushed sand and gravel into a sewer basin and clogged up the line. So sorry. They were very apologetic. The city sent two crews to clean out the sewer backup and help Mrs. J. clean up the mess in her house. They also sent over a city claims examiner to take pictures of the dismal scene and prepare a damage survey. The local newspaper carried a story of the incident. A few days later, at the request of the city claims examiner, Mrs. J. prepared and submitted to him a detailed list, complete with cost estimate of the ruined carpets, buckled floors, destroyed clothing, and messed up and smelly furniture and furnishings. The city attorney discussed the whole matter with Mrs. J. He was very nice and polite and haggled in a courteous way over the next few months. During all that time he was very correct; he could not have been more pleasant. But he did not bother to tell Mrs. J. about the ninety-day notice of claim law; after all, he was not *her* lawyer. Finally, by October, Mrs. J. got fed up with all the negotiating and wrote to the mayor complaining about the city's failure to satisfy her, detailing her claims, describing all the damages and the events, and estimating the cost. Dead silence being the only response, Mrs. J. brought suit against the city. The city attorney, as was his sworn duty, contested the action on the ground—guess what?—that Mrs. J.'s written claim to the mayor was made too late. The State Supreme Court, agreeing with the city attorney and affirming the District Court and the Court of Appeals, said that anything short of a written claim to the mayor within ninety days after the occurrence required a dismissal of the suit. And Mrs. J. could not believe her ears!

Some notice of claim laws are so strictly applied that they require compliance regardless of whether the victim of municipal neglect, assault, or accident is left flat on his back in the hospital or is out of his mind. Excuses for noncompliance generally fall upon deaf ears. The best advice I can give the victim of municipal negligence is to make sure to serve *timely* and proper notice, or get a lawyer *immediately,* preferably one familiar with local requirements. If you are in no condition to do it yourself, find somebody, a relative, a friend, the fellow in the next bed, to do it for you. Write down the details of the accident—date, time of day or night, place, and description. If you receive a head injury or even some other shock inducing injury, you may not remember the actual impact because of a phenomenon known as posttraumatic amnesia. But do the best you can.

There are many examples of the notice of claim gambit. For instance, a school child was rendered quadraplegic after a trampoline accident in a poorly supervised physical education class. The Idaho Supreme Court dismissed the child's case against the city educational authorities because a timely notice of claim had not been filed. The court said that neither infancy nor total disability excused noncompliance with the notice of claim law.

A man had parts of both legs amputated by mistake in a municipal hospital in Minnesota. To cover up what had happened, the municipal employees told him that his legs were gangrenous as a result of diabetes. As soon as he discovered the actual cause of his amputation—but more than sixty days after the surgery—he served a notice of claim for malpractice and sued. The Minnesota Supreme Court threw his case out for failure to serve a notice of claim promptly.

A lady was severely injured after a fall on a defective sidewalk in Detroit. She was taken home by a stranger—she lived alone—then brought to a hospital, "completely disoriented." She was soon "adjudged mentally incompetent"—all as a result of the accident. The city police were promptly informed of the accident and its consequences. The woman's court-appointed guardian served a notice of claim shortly after he was designated. It was rejected as filed too late, and the suit was dismissed by the Michigan courts. They held that police notification was insufficient, and declared the notice of claim law applicable even if a person had been rendered incompetent by the city's negligence.

A man was seriously hurt by the city's negligence and, seemingly in compliance with a state statute requiring service of notice of claim on a municipal officer within fourteen days after the accident, had a proper notice served within fourteen days on the city treasurer, certainly a significant city official. Unfortunately for the injured man, he did not know (who would?) that a different law defined a municipal officer in that city as "a member of the city council." And Maine's highest court rejected his suit because the notice was served on the wrong city official.

A citizen of Calhoun, Georgia had an experience she will not soon forget. She was seriously injured when a defect in the highway forced her car off a city road. She told the Calhoun city clerk about the accident a few days later. The Calhoun mayor and the city clerk actually visited the site of the accident a short time later. The injured woman actually appeared before the Calhoun City Council to tell of the occurrence. The council actually told her it would act on her claim as soon as her physician sent in a report of her injuries. After this went on for seven months, she finally presented a written account of her accident and claim. During all her discussions with the city clerk, the mayor and the city council, nobody bothered to tell her about the six-month notice of claim ordinance. When she finally exhausted her patience and sued for her damages, the Georgia Supreme Court dismissed her complaint on the ground that she failed to comply with the six-month written notice of claim requirement.

But do not get talked out of making a claim—and suing— because of failure to send timely notice of claim. Rescue from this Draconian rule is on the way. For example, in New York State it recently became the victim of its own excesses. Horrible examples of misuse of the notice of claim law piled up, and the legislature was finally moved to modify the old oppressive law and make it more rational. The absurd minor technicalities have been deleted. Almost any excuse for a few days' tardiness is sufficient to permit late filing, and a person disabled by an accident has a reasonable time to comply with the new law. If the victim is an infant he has until age eighteen to ask the courts for permission to file a late notice.

This is an important protection for the average citizen since notice of claim is required by most municipalities in all tort cases. In New York State municipalities, for example, medical malpractice suits against physicians who provide medical care in municipal hospitals or institutions are also subject to notice of claim requirements, since the city is legally obligated to indemnify them against claims.

In other states, courts are moving to moderate the more oppressive requirements of technical compliance. But do not count on such future reforms. Make sure that a reasonably detailed—date, time, place, and occurrence—notice of claim is served as soon as possible and on the right official.

Strangely, in these days of expanding constitutional rights, courts have struck down notice of claim laws in only two of the fifty states.

How to File a Notice of Claim

Notice of claim laws generally require that the notice itself, which in many cases must be sworn to before a notary public, include only the name and address of the claimant and his attorney, if any; the nature of the claim; the time and place of the accident or event; the manner in which the claim arose; and, to the extent that can be determined at the time, the damages or injuries claimed to have been sustained. In other words, your notice should indicate what happened, where it happened, the date and approximate time when it happened, a general and broad description of your injuries, and this important phrase "plus injuries as yet unascertained." Make a copy of the notice for future reference.

Municipalities generally prepare their own notice of claim forms, which far exceed these statutory requirements; the one prepared by New York City, included in the appendix, is typical. Commonly, forms handed out by local governments require names of witnesses and their addresses, and the name and badge number of any notified police. They also demand information about medical treatment, hospital treatment, names of physicians, and other similar material. In addition, they generally require detailed employment information, including the amount of work and pay lost and detailed accounts of doctors' bills. *You do not have to supply this information and, as a matter of fact, you should not.* The additional information is requested not for your benefit, but for the benefit of the municipality. *If you use the municipality's form, strike out the irrelevant questions instead of merely leaving them unanswered.* Bear in mind that the information contained in the notice of claim may be used against you on cross-examination, and can provide the municipality with an advantage that it is not entitled to.

If you are a do-it-yourself addict, you will need guidance. Ask the city's attorney where the notice must be presented. Then inquire at the office, to which you have been referred, to check that it is in fact the proper place to present a notice of claim. Serve the claim in person and get a stamped receipt for it on your own copy of the notice. Better than all these instructions, get a lawyer, particularly one experienced in the practice of suing municipalities.

If your accident was serious enough to attract a police officer, he will have made a record of it, including names and identification of involved persons and witnesses, which will be available to you. Inquire at the local police precinct. If your accident involved a motor vehicle, there will also be a record in the state motor vehicle office. You can generally get a copy for a small charge. These records will be useful in framing a proper notice of claim.

Here is a simple notice of claim form for an accident injury:

NOTICE OF CLAIM

I hereby make claim against the City of Light for injuries sustained by me.

My name is Jane Doe.

I live at 217 Main Street, Light, N.M.

My injury occurred at about 3 P.M. on July 4, 1980.

A City of Light owned and operated Department of Public Works truck knocked me down while I was crossing Main Street at Juniper Road in the City of Light.

My injuries, as far as I know at present, are a fractured left leg, several broken ribs, head injuries, concussion, contusions, abrasions, and severe physical and emotional shock.

JANE DOE, being duly sworn, says:

I am the claimant named in this claim; I have read it and know its contents; it is true to my knowledge.

(Signed) Jane Doe

Sworn to before me this
10th day of July, 1980.

_____

Alfred E. Smith,
Notary Public

The following is a typical property damage claim:

NOTICE OF CLAIM

I hereby make claim against the City of Nowork for damage to my property.

My name is John Doe.

I live at 100 Broadway, Nowork, N.J.

The front wall and porch of my house at 100 Broadway was caused to collapse when a Cadillac limousine owned by the City of Nowork and driven by an official of such city, its mayor, at an excessive speed, mounted the sidewalk and struck the front wall and porch.

The incident occurred and the damage was caused at approximately 3 A.M. on January 1, 1981.

The property damage, as presently known by me, consists of a demolished porch and front wall of my house, wrecked furniture and furnishing, consequential weakening of the house foundation, torn up lawn, destroyed trees, bushes, and flower beds, and other property damage associated with the occurrence.

JOHN DOE, being duly sworn, says:

I am the claimant named in this claim; I have read it and know its contents; it is true to my knowledge.

(Signed) John Doe

Sworn to before me this
10th day of January, 1981.

_____

Alfred E. Smith,
Notary Public

In each instance, if an attorney has been retained, his name must be included.

The Prior Notice Snare

So far, we have dealt only with the kind of notice that must be filed *after* the accident. Believe it or not, some municipalities require that, in addition, they receive written notice *before* the accident! For example, many cities and villages in New York State have prior notice laws. According to these laws, in order to sue for an accident on a sidewalk that a city or village has failed to make safe in winter weather —that is, free from dangerous, neglected accumulations of snow and ice—written notice of the condition must have been filed with the designated officials forty-eight hours or more *before* the accident for which you are claiming damages! Other dangerous, accident-generating local street and highway conditions—potholes, uneven sidewalks, sharp declivities, broken fences, toe traps, and others—also must have been called to the city's attention by written prior notice to give local government sufficient time to correct the defective condition. If prior notice has *not* been given, the injured citizen is left to nurse his sore rump or broken leg or repair his broken axle in uncompensated misery.

From a practical standpoint, prior notice is universally required in all cities, whether or not a prior notice law actually exists. The injured party must be able to prove that the street or other defect was one that local officials either knew about or should have known about because the condition had been in existence for so long. The difference is that in prior notice localities, actual *written* notice is required. In all other municipalities, written notice isn't necessary, but the injured party must be able to prove knowledge or the presumption of knowledge.

The application of various local prior notice ordinances can make your hair stand on end. For example, Buffalo, New York has one that brooks no variation or avoidance. There was a severe depression in a city roadway. When passing trucks and buses went over it, the surrounding buildings were literally shaken to their foundations until they were seriously damaged. The city engineer was formally notified in writing, and there was not the slightest doubt that the condition was not merely known to the city but was notorious. The property owners' suit for damages was dismissed because, if you please, the prior notice ordinance said that it had to be served on the city clerk, who had nothing to do with street maintenance. Instead, it had been served on the city engineer, who had everything to do with street maintenance.

In 1979, the city administration submitted a proposed local law to the New York City Council, which, in effect, exempts the city from all liability for accidents resulting from defects, obstructions, and unsafe conditions in sidewalks, roadways, park paths, public places, bridges, viaducts, wharves, boardwalks, underpasses, and public parking areas unless the city received written notice addressed to a specified city official, and the city did not take care of the condition within fifteen days. The fact that the city knew of the condition, the fact that the victim was a stranger to the area where the accident occurred, or was an infant, a foreigner, insane or simply unaware would make no difference. If written notice was not actually given, the victim would be out of luck, and the city would be home free.

The bill, quietly introduced during the early summer, was expected to suffer the fate of similar bills that had been submitted in the state legislature and the city council, year after year, and had been generally ignored. This one had different sponsors—the city's top elected officials—and it was, without any fanfare, scheduled for committee consideration in midsummer with the expectation that it would be speeded out of committee and passed by the council before opposition could be formed. But news of the bill and the proposed council committee meeting leaked out, and so numerous were those wanting to be heard—particularly in opposition— that a second and third hearing was held, and each ran all day until late evening.

The main argument against the bill, which is equally applicable to similar ordinances in other New York localities,[1]

---

1. Interestingly, such ordinances seem to be a New York phenomenon, not common elsewhere.

was that it was not really a prior notice requirement but an *immunity* law. Furthermore, considering the fact that there are 65,000 street blocks in the city, 6,000 miles of roads, 13,500 miles of sidewalks, hundreds of miles of boardwalk, thousands of miles of park paths, parkways and pedestrian areas, numerous bridges and many city parking areas (in which, incidentally, the city charges fees), it is obvious that prior notice of defects in such a multitude of areas could not be complied with to any effective degree. Added to the massive dimensions of compliance is the obvious fact that once notice is given there would be no way of taking into account weekly, daily, and even hourly changes in reported conditions. Thus, notices would have to be kept current, making a difficult task totally impossible. Finally, the city admits that it cannot keep up with necessary roadway, bridge, sidewalk, and other such repairs. Thus, even if it was practical to give notice, the end result would not change, except possibly to generate more accident claims. But after arm twisting by the mayor, to a degree never before seen at City Hall, the bill passed by a vote of twenty-four to sixteen. A movement is now under way by community groups and associations to organize a continuing campaign of prior notice-giving, and the City's attorney reports that "a blitz of defects . . . is overwhelming the City."

Whether the existing prior notice laws and ordinances of villages and cities can survive a new constitutional challenge under present-day notions of equal protection and due process is at least doubtful. The courts of Arizona, Mississippi, Oklahoma, Texas, and the state of Washington have invalidated such prior notice laws. New York might do the same some day. Persons severely injured in roadway and sidewalk accidents in prior notice localities might still have a fighting chance to recover damages, even if no required prior written notice was given to the locality. A small city in Minnesota added a prior notice provision to its charter, and the state legislature was so outraged at the notion that it enacted a state statute invalidating the provision and prohibiting the enactment of any such requirements by any locality. A person injured by a road defect in the city in question while the charter provision was in effect even got help from the Minnesota courts. They held the city officials responsible for repairing the highways *personally* liable—a decision that effectively ended that chapter in the city's litigation history. A singular Oregon Supreme Court decision resulted in the repeal of such local ordinances in that state.

Villages in New York—and some of them are larger than many cities—are immune from liability for defective village streets, highways, parking fields, and for accidents on golf courses and in parks unless the complainant can prove that the village clerk actually received prior *written* notice of the defects that caused the accident. There is a catch-22 aspect to this. If a person injured in a sidewalk or road defect accident proves he gave prior notice of the defect, he automatically admits to his own negligence in not avoiding a known danger. This admission can operate to reduce or defeat his claim. So, if you notice a hazardous defect and your crystal ball tells you that you are going to have an accident, get somebody else to notify the authorities.

Nevertheless, do not let city people talk you out of claiming—and suing—if you have been injured by a road or sidewalk defect or an accumulation of snow and ice, even though you cannot prove compliance with a prior notice law. A prior notice may actually have been filed. You can only be sure after you have questioned city officials. In your formal complaint you can allege "upon information and belief" that a prior notice exists and examine the city officials under oath. If there is a freedom of information law in the state (see chapter XI) you can require a search of the records. In New York, city and village clerks are required to keep and to make available to the public an indexed record of every such notice filed with them. But here is the catch: if they do not keep such records or make them available, that does not have any effect on a suit for street defects. You still have to prove prior notice.

There is not a great deal you can do to protect yourself against prior notice requirements, but you may be able to help others and others may be able to help you. As a good citizen, if you see a defective sidewalk, roadway, or other hazardous area, which might cause an accident, drop a postcard to the city clerk, town clerk, or village clerk, depending upon the location of the defect. If a sufficient number of good citizens do this, persons hurt by government neglect in prior notice municipalities may be compensated for their injuries, and local officials will be warned to take proper steps to correct the defects in order to prevent people from getting hurt and suing the locality.

A post card notice can be simple:

NOTICE OF DEFECTIVE STREET

You are hereby notified that there is a serious defective condition (or dangerous accumulation of snow and ice) on the sidewalk in front of 127 Main Street. Please forward this Notice to the appropriate official.

July 4, 1980   Citizen

If possible, ask the city attorney (or village or town attorney) which official should receive the notice. In several cities in New York State, for example, the commissioner of public works must be notified of a sidewalk, street, or other defect.

The courts in some states are almost as annoyed as you are about these crazy laws and occasionally will bend over backwards to get around them. For instance, service of written notice is not required if the dangerous street condition was actually created by the city: if, for example, the ice you slipped on resulted from fire department activity at a burning building and was allowed to remain for several days; or if the accident was caused by a loose manhole cover installed by the city water department. Any street condition actually created by the city, or under its direction, which causes an accident, will generally excuse compliance with a prior notice law and permit suit against the city.

Starting a Suit

There are almost always special statutes of limitation on municipal suits. In other words, municipalities set a specific limit on the time you have to institute a suit after the right to sue arises. And they always shorten that period. For example, the usual length of time for suit on an accident claim is three years; on a commercial agreement it is six years. But, the common period for any suit against a city is one year. On contract claims cities often shorten that period to six months. There are also prescribed limits on how *soon* you can sue a city; usually not earlier than thirty to sixty days after you make a claim on the city. And this applies to all kinds of suits for personal injuries, for damage to property, and on contracts.

Therefore, if you sue too soon, your action will be dismissed, and you will have to start it all over again. If you sue too late, then you are out of luck altogether.

The principle to follow is simple and important. Assert your claim against the municipality—whether it is for an accident or a business deal—as soon as you have a right to make a claim. Then, particularly if your claim is based on a business deal or contract with a municipality (see chapter VIII), you can negotiate a settlement with some feeling of security. And do not let vital time go by before suing. Remember, too, it is easier to get a settlement before a court of law and an impartial judge than it is all alone before a local bureaucrat, who probably has very limited authority to make binding decisions.

IN SUMMARY

If you sustain injury or your property is damaged, follow these six steps:

1. **If it is a sidewalk, roadway, or similar situation, check to see if a prior notice was filed. If not, go ahead with your suit anyway. The laws are so arbitrary that the courts may very well find in your favor.**

2. **Prepare notice of claim. Have it notarized, and make a copy for yourself.**

3. **Take the notice of claim down to the city, town, or village attorney and ask him where it must be filed.**

4. **File the notice of claim in the proper place. Get a stamped receipt on your own copy. Alternatively, retain a lawyer to take care of items one through three and you will feel safer.**

5. **In most localities, the law requires the claimant to promptly appear, on demand, for both a physical examination and questioning under oath. If the local government demands that you appear for examination and questioning, do not ignore the notice no matter how abrupt (or polite) it is. Ignoring such a notice may forfeit your claim!**

6. **Do not wait too long to start suit. Usually you have to give the locality thirty days or so to think it over. Soon after that bring suit to avoid being barred from suing by a statute of limitations. One year is the usual time limit.**

CHAPTER III

Assorted Suits
Against the City

As a GENERAL RULE, municipalities can be sued for motor vehicle accidents, even—except in the few states with strict sovereign immunity—those involving police cars and fire department trucks, and for the sort of negligence for which people are generally liable to suit. Typically, a city that operates a hospital is liable for medical malpractice. It can be sued for accidents on municipal golf courses or in city housing projects, or for accidents resulting from defective stairways and elevators in its public buildings. If it operates a zoo, a city is liable if a lion escapes and eats a citizen. For the most part, a city, like a private person or corporation, is subject to all the common ills and risks of our complex and danger-infested society.

This chapter will cover the municipal governmental activities that entail, seem to entail, or should entail responsibility for injury to persons and property—even the kinds of suit generating occurrences that people often assume nobody, least of all the local government, is liable for.

Street and Sidewalk Accidents

A municipality is obliged to maintain its sidewalks in good condition. For instance, if a sidewalk is unsafe—a projecting manhole cover, radically uneven flagstones, or collapsed areas—a city is liable to a pedestrian who breaks his leg or neck on that unsafe sidewalk. Yet, funny, irrational rules occasionally develop even in such simple matters. For a long time it was an accepted rule in New York that unless a sidewalk defect was more than four inches in depth there could be no suit against the municipality. The so-called four-inch rule was "as strong as proof of holy writ." Some negligence lawyers in New York employed photographers who would guarantee to produce pictures of one-half-inch sidewalk declivities that looked like the Grand Canyon. Actually, four inches is about the thickness of the one-volume Columbia Encyclopedia, and it was plain silly to apply such a rule to persons seriously injured by falling over a three-and-one-half-inch sidewalk projection at night on a poorly lit street. Finally, an alert lower court judge rejected the four-inch rule, and he was sustained by New York's highest court, which blandly noted that there never was such a rule.

Sidewalk accidents are a common event in the lives of city dwellers. New York City, which has more than 13,500 miles of sidewalks—certainly at least ten percent of which (1,350 miles) are in bad shape—pays out more than $5½ million in claims for injuries resulting from defective sidewalk pavements. And that is only a minor part of the actual damage suffered by injured pedestrians, most of whom either do not bother or do not know enough to sue the city.

But all this is subject to whatever prior notice laws exist in the locality where the injury occurred. However, remember that you can check to see if such prior notice was received, and if it was, you can institute a suit *after* filing a notice of claim.

A suit was brought on behalf of a youngster who was seriously injured while skating on a defective city sidewalk. A persuasive city attorney convinced the court that since sidewalks, as the name implies, are for walking, not for skating, the city was not liable. But do not let this dissuade you from making a claim in a similar situation. That kind of argument might not work the next time.

As a matter of fact, another judge of the same court came to the opposite conclusion, saying, "For the city to claim that rollerskating is an unusual and extraordinary use of its sidewalks, which it did not and was not expected to contemplate is absurd."

A city also must keep local street traffic signals and stop signs in working condition and properly in place. If an accident results from a defect in or absence of proper signs, the city is liable.

One New Year's Eve, a late-night celebrant, woozy and feeling no pain, drove his car down a dead-end street through a barrier and into the river. The postmortem revealed a heavy concentration of alcohol in his brain. At first it seemed obvious that the accident was nobody's fault but the victim's. But it was discovered that a state law required placement of a lighted warning sign twenty feet before the end of a street leading into a river. Furthermore, there is a rule of law favoring the claimant in a death action and placing the burden of proof on the defendant. In other words, the defendant had to prove the accident was entirely the fault of the dead man. And since the proof clearly indicated that the dead-end sign was not illuminated, the widow was comforted by a substantial judgment against the city.

The Perils of Good Citizenship

There is another peculiar aspect to street and sidewalk accidents. Generally, local ordinances require a property owner to clear, clean, and make safe the sidewalk in front of his store, factory, home, and so on. If he fails to do so and a person breaks his neck on his defective or frozen walk, that does not necessarily make him liable. The liability is still the city's. In most places, the worst that can happen to the property owner is a slap-on-the-wrist small fine. But, if good citizen property owner defectively repairs or clears snow from his sidewalk and somebody trips on the defect or slips on the icy residue and breaks a leg, then—guess what?—the good citizen is liable, because, say the courts, he created the dangerous condition. Moral: good citizenship is not all it is cracked up to be. Virtue has its own rewards and punishments. But there is an advantage in this type of situation for the injured person. In a suit against the property owner, neither the prior notice requirement nor the notice of claim law applies. So that action against the property owner does not have the built-in traps peculiar to suits against municipalities. And the chances are that he carries liability insurance that will assure you of a source of payment for your injuries.

Legal Assistance

If you decide to retain an attorney to handle the case, arrange for the legal fees on a contingency basis. Here are a few examples of contingency fees in such accident cases:

New York: 50% of the first $1,000; 40% of the next $2,000; 35% of the next $20,000; 25% of all amounts over $25,000; occasionally, a flat 33⅓% is fixed

New Jersey: 33⅓% of the first $50,000; 20% of the next $50,000; and 10% of anything over $100,000

Illinois: 33⅓%; if settled before trial, 25%

In California, the contingency fee would be $141,667 on $1,000,000. And on that same amount in Michigan, the fee would be either $162,250 or $183,333 depending on the applicable schedule. In most states "fair and reasonable" is the measure applied by the courts. You can always negotiate with your lawyer for a lower-than-scale fee, but do not pay more than scale. The local bar association can tell you what the going rate is.

IN SUMMARY

1. Cities, towns, villages, and counties are liable for accidents resulting from defective streets, roads, sidewalks, and public ways (subject to whatever prior notice laws exist). That includes potholes that crack axles, cause cars to swerve and smash walls, shops, and people. It also includes defective traffic signals that cause accidents.

2. Sidewalks are for people, not for bicycles, skateboards, or cars. Do not expect to be successful if you are hurt by those kinds of activities, but do not give up too quickly. Consult a lawyer.

3. Get your notice of claim in fast and sue as soon as you are permitted to.

4. Do not resist examination by the defendant, but remember that the government lawyer is not on your side.

5. If you decide to clear off snow and ice or repair the sidewalk in front of your house, make sure you do a good job or you will risk being sued if somebody is hurt by a condition you create.

Hidden Hurts and Damages

Do not underestimate the seriousness of injuries or the extent of property damage that seemingly minor accidents can cause.[1] A fall on an icy or defective sidewalk, from

---

1. This is why the addition of the phrase discussed on page 29, or a variation thereof, in your notice of claim is so important.

which the victim walks away with hardly any apparent injury but to his dignity, can later turn out to be really serious. Potholes not only jar teeth, but, like sidewalk falls, can dislocate and shatter small bones and injure muscles and tendons. Such accidents can have what negligence lawyers, borrowing from physicians, call sequelae—not originally noticed but quite severe. Even damages to a car from a pothole can have initially unnoticed sequelae—out-of-whack steering, displaced radiators, misaligned wheels, and other problems—which result in whopping repair bills. Actual damages are far more common than claims for such damages. Even so, particularly in large cities, claims against the municipality for broken axles, cracked wheels, and smashed rear ends run into very large sums of money. In a single bad year for potholes New York City paid out half a million dollars for such claims. There are many cases on the books in which the time limit on serving a notice of claim has run out before the full magnitude of injuries and damages manifested itself, and the victim lost his chance to sue the municipality.

What might seem to be a minor injury can turn out to be major—even fatal. A headache that became tolerable after a while, led to a diagnosis of subdural hematoma with disabling and close to fatal results six months later—the result of a low-speed collision between a city truck and a car. In another example, a man phoned his doctor for advice on what to take for headaches. The doctor knew the caller was a tightwad who was avoiding an office visit, so he asked no questions, gave the man a fast brush-off, and told him to take two aspirins. Some months later the man died. His death was the end result of the skull fracture he had received when he slipped on a defective sidewalk. He had not told his doctor about the accident, nor had his doctor bothered to ask. In both cases, no notice of claim had been served on the city because the victims thought their injuries too slight to bother about, and it was too late to do so when the seriousness of the case became apparent.

Donna Wernett of Onondaga County, New York was more fortunate. A county snow plow backed into her car. Mrs. Wernett assumed that only the car was damaged and she accepted $688 for repairs from the county's insurance carrier. Six months later she was flat on her back in the hospital. The slight discomfort she noticed after the accident developed into a very serious injury—a bilateral thoracic outlet syndrome—requiring two separate surgical operations. In almost any other state the municipality would have been free of liability for failure to file a ninety-day notice of claim promptly. But, as noted, New York has a special liberal law, and Mrs. Wernett was permitted to sue and obtain a substantial award.

IN SUMMARY

There is no certainty that an injury is minor. If your head is hurt, or your eye affected, or your back out of kilter, for example, do not ignore it. The old adage "What you don't know, won't hurt you," is totally wrong. See a doctor. And don't resist a suggestion of X ray. Even strong people are made of flesh and bone and blood and muscle. What seems like nothing can be serious indeed.

And do not forget the ten- or thirty- or ninety-day notice of claim requirement.

Parks and Playgrounds

In maintaining parks, playgrounds, and swimming pools, municipalities involve themselves in extensive liability. For example, a city is liable if it fails to provide a nonskid diving board and a swimmer slips and breaks his neck. A swimmer who entered a municipal lake area at 2:00 A.M. and seriously injured himself diving into a shallow area of the lake from a diving board recovered a large judgment against the municipality for negligent supervision, control, and construction of the facility. Similarly, a young man who dove off a municipal recreation pier into shallow water and consequently became a quadraplegic recovered a judgment from the municipality.

Municipal parks and playgrounds must be maintained in a reasonably safe condition, and some degree of supervision should be provided, particularly when the facilities are used by children. A pack of stray dogs was known to congregate in a playground, and one of them bit a child who fell and hurt himself, resulting in a suit against the municipality and a substantial recovery.

A lakeside municipal beach had a floating diving dock. The municipality allowed speed boats to use the area and did not bother to post warning signs to guide the swimmers or the speed boat owners. A little girl who was swimming was struck by a speeding boat, knocked unconscious, and drowned. The child's parents successfully sued the local government.

Recently, after an incomplete six day trial, the city of Philadelphia, Pennsylvania agreed to pay $1,800,000 to settle a suit brought on behalf of a child who came so close to drowning in a city swimming pool that he suffered severe paralysis and loss of speech. The basis of the claim was the absence of a sufficient number of lifeguards at the pool.

A young gang used a city playground as its *turf,* and the local police did nothing about it in spite of citizen complaints. One day the gang set upon a young boy and injured him severely. The city was successfully sued and had to pay substantial damages.

A fireworks display in a county park got out of hand.

Rockets landed and exploded in the middle of a crowd of children. The county was held liable for the serious injuries that resulted.

Trampolines in playgrounds and school gyms are potential cripplers of young people. Injuries from unsupervised or poorly supervised trampoline activities are shockingly common, and courts and juries have awarded large verdicts to trampoline accident victims in such situations.

It is not uncommon for people to assume that if there is an element of self-blame involved in an accident, there is no basis for a claim or suit for injuries. A group of children went onto a railroad track adjacent to a city park and decided that it would be fun to race a slow freight train. One of them slipped under the wheels of the caboose and was badly hurt. The child's parents were sure that the accident was the kid's own fault because he had no right to be on the railroad track chasing trains. But an alert lawyer got a substantial award for the lad. His argument, which satisfied the judge and jury, was based on the fact that railroad tracks and freight trains are particularly attractive to small boys. Since the city should have known that kids using the park would stray onto the track, they should have securely fenced it off.

In another situation, a railroad cut adjacent to a city sidewalk was protected by a ten-foot-high chain link fence. But over the years the edge of the sidewalk had worn away, and children had dug out enough space to crawl through and climb down onto the tracks. A small child did just that, and slid under a moving freight train. Again, although the parents thought it was nobody's fault but little Johnny's, they were put straight and received a substantial judgment. Having fenced off the track, the city had a duty to maintain it, so as not to invite adventurous small boys to crawl through and put themselves in danger.

IN SUMMARY

If you get hurt in a city, village, park, playground, or golf-course, or by recreational equipment or roughnecks, assume that you have the right to sue. Children are generally attracted to interesting places, and if they are not protected areas it is to be expected that children will seek them out. If your child is injured in such an area, do not blame the kid, sue the city.

Ambulance Service

In a suburban New York town a resident got undressed and took a nap after a hard morning of shoveling snow. He was awakened in the middle of his pleasant dreams by his wife, who announced that there was a leak underneath the kitchen sink. Naked and half asleep, he staggered downstairs and crawled under the sink where the family cat was taking its own nap. Very much annoyed, the cat reached up and scratched him in the most available place. He brought his head up in shock, banged it against the underside of the sink, and was out cold. His wife called the municipal ambulance. The attendants loaded the unconscious resident on a stretcher and started to move him down the pathway. He awoke and said, "Where am I?" The ambulance attendant asked him what had happened, and his answer so amused one of the stretcher-bearers that he laughed and dropped his end of the stretcher. The result was a suit against the municipality for one broken leg and hurt feelings.

In another case, a call for a city ambulance for a heart attack victim was ignored for an hour. The citizen died and the city was sued.

A city ambulance in service may go through a red light. But if it does so without sounding its siren and collides with another car, the city will be held responsible for the injuries inflicted. Many cities do operate ambulance services. If you are injured in any way by negligence on their part, you do have the right to sue.

Police Activity—and Inactivity

Police action or non-action, particularly the non-criminal or nonviolent kind that occurs in the course of law enforcement, is a constant and often neglected source of local government litigation. Late at night two police officers in a small city responded to a radio call to their patrol car and picked up a couple of boisterous, befuddled drunks. In accordance with standard operating procedure the officers drove them out of town to an abandoned golf course and left them to dry out in Stygian darkness. About 350 feet from the spot where the men were abandoned there was an active limited-access highway, and the drunks could hear the humming and buzzing of the speeding traffic in the distance. "In their befuddled state," an appeals court was later to say, "the men lost little time responding to its siren song." They straggled toward its source, ambled onto the speedway, and were soon knocked down by an astonished motorist.

Now do not get the idea that it was the drunks' own fault and that if they had not been picked up they might well have fallen into a ditch or off the sidewalk or been run down ambling along the middle of a city roadway. In this case they were well advised; they sued the city and recovered a judgment. For, said the court, a drunk may not be "run out of town" by the police, nor may they abandon him in a strange uncharted place and leave him to the perils of the darkness. A drunk is not an outlaw, nor is he somebody to be played with. The duty of the police was to take him into custody if he was causing a disturbance, and if not, to at least refrain from increasing the normal dangers inherent in drunken helplessness.

Here is another example that shows the cop as bureaucrat, bound in red tape by rules and regulations not of his own making. The following verbatim account is taken directly from the opinion of a New York court:

On May 6, 1977, Robert Susser purchased a 1969 Chrysler Imperial automobile. On July 1, 1977, Mr. Susser legally parked his car on an upper west side Manhattan street. On July 2, 1977, Mr. Susser discovered his car was gone.

Mr. Susser reported the theft to the 24th police precinct at once and was told that an alarm describing the stolen vehicle would be communicated to other police precincts. The police cautioned Mr. Susser that in the unlikely event he located the car he was to call them immediately and not attempt to move it himself.

On the morning of July 3, Mr. Susser prevailed upon his friend, Richard Cotton, to delay a trip to Massachusetts and canvass the local streets with him in search of the Chrysler. As they were about to abandon their efforts, they discovered the automobile parked on Manhattan Avenue between 109th and 110th Streets.

As instructed, Mr. Susser called the 24th precinct immediately. While waiting for the police to arrive, he entertained visions of police officers dusting the car for fingerprints and traps being laid to apprehend the thieves. But no police personnel arrived. Mr. Susser then dialed 911. Still no police. Again and again he called 911. No police.

Exasperated, he dispatched Mr. Cotton to the 24th precinct while he remained to guard the car. During Mr. Cotton's absence, Mr. Susser flagged down a passing police car and told the officer his tale of woe. Mr. Susser then opened the door of the Chrysler and the officer was able to observe that the ignition switch had been punched out and replaced with a phony switch.

The officer then requested that Mr. Susser accompany him to the 24th precinct in order to fill out various police forms and to "clear" the alarm which had been previously communicated to other police officers throughout the city. Mr. Susser questioned the wisdom of this plan and asked who would safeguard the car in their absence. The police officer removed the coil wire and assured Mr. Susser that the car would remain inoperable. Unpersuaded, Mr. Susser stated his intention to stay with his Chrysler and suggested that the officer "clear the alarm" on his squad car radio. The officer refused, explaining that the alarm had to be cleared at the precinct. Mr. Susser was told that he could not take possession of his car until the alarm was cleared and the proper police forms completed.

Mr. Susser was again directed to go to the precinct with the officers, which he did. At the precinct, Mr. Cotton, already very late, left for Massachusetts. Mr. Susser was told to wait. After a while, he asked why he had to wait so long. He was informed that it sometimes takes up to three hours to clear an alarm. Mr. Susser bolted from the precinct, and, accompanied by a mechanic from his local garage, returned to Manhattan Avenue to reclaim his car. The car was gone.

The City of New York apparently based its defense in this lawsuit upon the officer's judgment that removing the coil wire would render the car inoperable. Coil wires are to car thieves as sneakers are to burglars. Any reasonable person could have foreseen, as Mr. Susser did, that a car thief would be undeterred by the removal of a coil wire.

No acceptable explanation was advanced for the requirement that the alarm be cleared only at the precinct. Even more incredible was the justification offered by the police for refusing to permit Mr. Susser to assume custody of the car while the alarm was outstanding. It was suggested that another officer might mistake Mr. Susser for the car thief and injure him or an innocent bystander. Mr. Susser was prepared to engage a mechanic to start the car and drive it, with a police escort, to the precinct or to a garage. This involved no risk to anyone. The course of action taken by the police was unnecessary and unreasonable.

Police in Hot Pursuit

The police are required to pursue and arrest law violators, including those who disobey traffic regulations, and the city is *not* liable if a police car collides with another vehicle during such pursuit. However, police officers do not have a license to be careless in these situations. For example, police were in hot pursuit of a driver who had gone through a stop light. In response to a radio alert from a pursuing police car, a roadblock was set up on a narrow suburban road. A truck driver, unaware of the situation, suddenly found his way blocked at the foot of a hill and before he could divert his truck into a hedge, the pursued vehicle, traveling at high speed, came over the hill. The resulting collision caused major injuries. A jury verdict for the truck driver victim was upheld as proper because it was proved that positioning the police car as a roadblock on wet pavement on a narrow road was contrary to sensible police practice.

It is not unusual for juries, aided by the testimony of experienced former traffic police, to second-guess police officers on the propriety of placing roadblocks in the path of escaping law breakers in speeding cars. And verdicts imposing liability on cities in such cases are not uncommon. Failure to sound a siren or to turn on flashing lights is a fairly common cause of serious accidents by police in pursuit of criminals. And although police are only required to use their judgment in such situations, juries are not likely to leave a victim uncompensated for terrible injuries. They tend to balance their view of the correctness of the police action against the reality of a severely injured plaintiff.

The Right to Police Service

Is there a right to police protection? It depends. A person injured by police action or inaction may or may not be entitled to an award depending upon differences in circumstances that seem irrational to anyone except a law professor or an appellate judge. First, let us look at a few typical situations and try to work out some rational guidelines for municipal liability in cases involving police action or inaction. However, be warned, it is almost impossible to develop a rational classification in this area. Nowhere else is the sentiment expressed by Mr. Bumble in Charles Dickens' *Oliver Twist* more apt, "Then I say, the Law is a ass!"

Consider the following four cases. In the first case, a riot was brewing on a pier when it was discovered that forged tickets for an excursion had been distributed, and people who had bought legitimate tickets were being turned back. The city sent one lone patrolman to deal with the very tense situation, and the result was that scores of people were trampled, some fatally. Claims for damages were rejected.

In the second case, a child was raped and mugged near a housing project that had a notorious reputation for violence that was well known to the police. Again, a claim for damages was rejected.

In a third bizarre case, a love-crazed rejected suitor had his beloved blinded with lye. The victim had pleaded for protection and warned the police of the imminence of an attack, but they did nothing about it. The claim for compensation was rejected. (There is a curious footnote to this: after the love-crazed suitor got out of jail, he married his blinded beloved and they lived happily ever after.)

And in a final example, a crazy sniper in a tower overlooking a busy thoroughfare killed two people and injured a number of others. The police had full notice of the situation and did not bother to cordon off the area. A motorist stopped his car when the horn went out of control. Unaware that the malfunction had been caused by a bullet, he got out of his car to investigate. He was shot by the sniper. He too was denied recovery.

In each case the reasoning, expressed in legalese, was the same. According to the courts, the duty of a local government to provide police protection is one owed to the entire community, not to separate individuals. So if the municipality fails to perform that duty, the individual citizen has no right to sue. This is known as the rule of police discretion. Here is a simple analogy: if a nation has incompetent generals who lose a war, it is the country, not just the individual citizen, that is hurt by the general's mistakes. The country's leaders can fire the general, but the citizen can not sue the country for any damage he suffered.

A woman who was assaulted and robbed in a subway station of a city rapid transit system, known to be the site of disorder and crime, recovered judgment on the ground that the city is actually in the railroad business and, like any other railroad operator, is obligated to protect passengers from known dangers.

A recent dramatic example was the case of the young music student who was shoved onto the tracks of a subway station of the New York City Transit System. Her hand was amputated, but miraculously reattached by skilled city surgeons. But her career as a flautist was ended. Suit is pending for the very drastic damages suffered.

New York City's mounted police have a reputation for skilled crowd control. The mounts are specially trained and seem to have a special kind of horse sense in treading lightly and moving gently. But recently, a mountie came up against a crowd of a few thousand young rock enthusiasts who jammed the sidewalk in front of a record shop where a popular rock star was autographing albums. Their activities confused the mountie and his horse as they moved in on the crowd. This resulted in a panic that sent the crowd of screaming youngsters up against and through the window of the shop. Fifty were injured, and the damage to the shop ran to about $50,000. And, of course, the city is being sued on the grounds that the mountie and/or the horse were inadequately trained. That too, makes a difference.

In one famous case, a man named Shuster pointed out an escaped convict, the famous bankrobber, Willie Sutton,[2] to the police and enjoyed considerable publicity—photo, interview, name, address, the works. Shortly after that, Shuster was shot and killed, presumably by an admirer of Sutton. The New York courts held that the city and its police owed a special duty to protect an informer and allowed suit by Shuster's estate.

A bystander negligently shot by a policeman in the course of a crime incident is entitled to sue. A taxi driver, shot by a holdup man who was arrested and placed in his cab by a policeman who forgot to disarm the prisoner, has a right to sue. The estate of an arrested man, who died from pneumonia in a stationhouse after he was tossed into an unheated cell with a fractured hip, is entitled to sue.

The estate of a man shot by a cop for making a disturbance while intoxicated has a right to damages because the cop obviously used unwarranted force. A woman shot by a husband to whom the police had negligently returned a pistol after being warned of his propensity for violence is entitled to damages. A bystander injured while directing traffic at the request of a policeman can sue. A person cannot be drafted

---

2. Willie was known for his wise observation that the reason he robbed banks was because "that's where the money is," a phenomenon recently rediscovered in New York City, with a consequent epidemic of bank robberies.

to perform a public service for which he is not properly trained.

In the following tragic case, a competent lawyer was able to prove such a particularly extreme instance of police neglect that the court was bound to find a basis upon which to permit an award. A woman was granted a certificate of protection by the family court that authorized any police officer to take her husband into custody if he threatened her. Repeated requests for police protection against violent threats from her husband were turned down. Subsequently, the husband took their child, stabbed her with a screwdriver, partially sawed off her leg, and slashed her from head to toe. A suit for permanent and severe injury inflicted on the child was upheld on the narrow ground that the woman's certificate of protection, which would have justified suit for injury to the wife in such circumstances, should be extended to cover the child. This needs more than this passing note, because it shows how extreme a case must be to induce the courts to award damages for failure to provide police protection.

Consider the studiously factual statement of a New York judge who refused to dismiss the claim for damages for the horribly mutilated child, but found it necessary to justify that decision in a detailed opinion stating the following facts:

> Prior to November 8, 1975, Frank Sorichetti was known to the defendant's police officers at the 43rd Precinct, having previously been arrested by them approximately six times for drunkenness, abusive and physical assault upon his family. Frank Sorichetti's police records, including his arrest and complaint records, maintained in the 43rd Precinct corroborated his vicious propensities and his prior assaults.
>
> In July 1975 Frank Sorichetti assaulted his wife with a knife, inflicting lacerations which required suturing at Jacobi Hospital; she thereafter brought a divorce

action, which resulted in further violence by Frank Sorichetti and threats by him that he would kill her and the children if she proceeded with the divorce action. Josephine Sorichetti thereupon went into the Family Court where, on September 18, 1975, she obtained a preliminary order of protection against her husband; thereafter, on November 6, 1975 the order was finalized for one year and, over her strenuous objections was amended to grant Frank Sorichetti visitation with Dina from 10:00 A.M. on Saturdays to 6:00 P.M. on Sundays. After the parties left the courtroom on November 6, Frank Sorichetti attempted to assault his wife and he had to be restrained by a court officer. The Family Court Judge was informed of the incident and thereupon directed the court officer to get Frank Sorichetti out of the building; however, the judge did not rescind Frank Sorichetti's weekend visitation with the infant.

In accordance with the provisions of the Family Court Act, a "Certificate of Order of Protection" was duly issued to Josephine Sorichetti by the clerk of that court on November 6, 1975 certifying that an order of protection had been issued to her, pursuant to which Frank Sorichetti was "forbidden to assault, menace, harass, endanger, threaten or act in a disorderly manner toward petitioner and . . . [he] is to remain away from the home of said petitioner."

The certificate issued to Josephine Sorichetti further recited, pursuant to statute: "AND IT IS PROVIDED BY LAW that the presentation of this Certificate to any Peace Officer shall constitute authority for said Peace Officer to take into custody the person charged with violating the terms of such Order of Protection and bring said person before this Court and otherwise, so far as lies within his power, to aid the Petitioner in securing the protection such Order was intended to afford."

As provided in said order of protection, Frank Sorichetti was directed to remain away from Josephine

Sorichetti's home and the parties were told by the Family Court that the infant was to be delivered and picked up at the 43rd Precinct.

Two days later, on Saturday, November 8, Josephine Sorichetti took the infant to the 43rd Precinct to accord Frank Sorichetti his weekend visitation. Frank Sorichetti took the infant and, as he was walking away, he made a death threat against his wife, Josephine Sorichetti, and the infant, Dina Sorichetti, and he indicated to Josephine that before the weekend was up she would be making "the sign of the cross" which to them meant that there would be a death. Josephine Sorichetti immediately went into the precinct and told the desk officer of the death threats to herself and the infant; she showed the desk officer the certificate of order of protection; she advised him of her fears and told him that she was frightened for the safety of her child and herself and that the order of protection protected her from such threats and she requested the police to take Frank Sorichetti into custody for violating said order. However, the police refused to do anything whatsoever.

The next day, Sunday, November 9, at 5:30 P.M., Josephine Sorichetti returned to the 43rd Precinct where she spoke successively to Police Officer Lo Bello and then to Lieutenant Granelo, and she reported to each of them the events of the day before, including the death threats by Frank Sorichetti against her daughter and herself; she told them of her fears and she showed each of them the certificate of order of protection issued to her by the Family Court. She repeated her demand that they arrest Frank Sorichetti for violation of the order of protection and that they dispatch a police car to his apartment to pick up the infant. The police again refused to do anything, telling her to wait outside for Frank Sorichetti to bring the infant back.

Frank Sorichetti failed to return the infant at 6:00 P.M., as required by the order of protection. Josephine

Sorichetti again went into the station house and she again spoke to Lo Bello and Granelo and she again demanded that the police arrest her husband for violating the order and protect the infant; once again the police refused to do anything whatsoever and Granelo told her to wait a couple of hours and that "perhaps" Frank Sorichetti had taken the infant to a movie. Josephine Sorichetti continued her vigil and continued to wait in front of the precinct. Thereafter, on three separate occasions she returned inside the precinct to plead with the police for help; on each occasion she repeated the threats against their lives which had been made by Frank Sorichetti, as well as repeating the various incidents and assaults previously perpetrated by him and each time she showed the police the certificate of order of protection, stating each time that the order of protection had been violated by Frank Sorichetti and each time demanding that the police act to protect the infant. The police continued their refusal to do anything. In fact, Lieutenant Granelo's response, after seeing the certificate was "So what, what have you got there, they mean nothing." Granelo, however, offered Josephine Sorichetti the gratuitous advice that in all probability the infant had been returned to her apartment. At about 6:30 P.M., one-half hour after Frank Sorichetti was required to but failed to return the infant, Granelo graciously permitted Sorichetti to use the precinct telephone to call home, where her girlfriend was waiting; the infant had not been returned and Josephine Sorichetti so informed Granelo and she again requested that the police send a car to Frank Sorichetti's apartment to pick up the infant and arrest Frank Sorichetti, but all to no avail. Josephine Sorichetti continued to wait at the precinct until about 7:00 P.M. and when the infant was not returned by then, Granelo advised her to go home and stay there and that in all probability the infant would be returned there. Josephine Sorichetti was finally convinced that the police would not comply with the command in the certificate of order of protection and would not do anything at all to assist her or to protect the infant and she returned home after leaving her telephone number with Granelo in the event of the infant was brought back to the precinct.

Thereafter, and sometime after 7:00 P.M., on November 9, Frank Sorichetti's sister entered his apartment at 2156 Cruger Avenue, which is located in the 43rd Precinct. She found him lying on the floor with an empty whiskey bottle and an empty pill bottle lying beside him. She also found the infant, who had been viciously attacked, mutilated and severely injured by her father and she telephoned the police. Sorichetti had attacked the infant at about 7:00 P.M. with a fork, a knife and screwdriver; he had attempted to saw her leg off with a saw; she had been slashed from head to toe and she had sustained severe multiple internal injuries. Minutes later police officers from the same 43rd Precinct arrived and they rushed the infant to Jacobi Hospital in their police car, without waiting for an ambulance; the infant was immediately taken into surgery and she was operated on until approximately 2:00 A.M. the following day. The infant was in a coma for several days and she remained in a critical condition for approximately three weeks and was hospitalized until December 19, 1975 (40 days). Dina Sorichetti remains severely and permanently disabled.

Frank Sorichetti was arrested after the attack on the infant and he was thereafter indicted by the Grand Jury, tried and found guilty of attempted murder of the infant and he is now serving a jail sentence for the crime.

Curiously, if there had been no certificate of protection issued to the mother, the city would have escaped all liability for the crass indifference of its police officials to the imminent danger threatening the child.

The city argued that the certificate of protection applied only to the mother and not the child, and since the victim was the child and not the mother, the usual police discretion rule barred the child's law suit. The court, hardly restraining its sense of outrage at the rule and its attempted application to the facts of the case, rejected the argument. So far the decision has been upheld by an intermediate appellate court.

Ironically, if almost any of the horrible examples of fault without liability described above had occurred in a city park or playground, damages would almost certainly have been awarded against the city on the ground that when a city establishes a place of recreation it is obliged to keep it safe and secure for those who use it. The distinction really does not make much sense, but there it is, at least for the time being, and until the courts modify their position.

A variation on this theme was recently provided by a New York court in circumstances that resemble a throwback to earlier colonial times—an Indian raid, no less, and the perils of travel through hostile territory in an area in the Adirondack Forest Preserve that an Indian tribe claimed as part of their reservation. The Indians turned the area into an armed encampment with a free-fire zone and bunkers. A family of settlers—that is vacationers—unaware that the Mohawks were on the war path, drove along a road into the area. Furthermore, they were not warned by the police, who knew what was going on. They were fired on by the Indians and one of them, a child, was seriously injured. The court awarded $150,000 damages on the ground that this was not merely the ordinary failure to provide general police protection. Specifically, the police had failed to keep a recreation area, owned and controlled by the state, safe and had further failed to maintain a road in that area in a reasonably secure condition after having been warned of a highly dangerous situation that required at least a roadblock and a patrol. Although the police in this case were state police, and the area was a state park, the same rule would apply to city police and a city park.

The person who gets arrested for drunk and disorderly conduct is actually better protected than the drunk who wanders off quietly by himself. The arrestee has the comfort of knowing that the police are bound to keep him from harm. And if they let him fall down and break his neck, the city is liable for damages. Not so the quiet lush; he can fall into a ditch or get himself run down on the highway, and nobody is held to be at fault but himself.

Hospitals are usually thought to be safe and secure. Mrs. Nelson, who went to a city hospital's dentistry clinic, certainly thought so. All she had was a small child with a toothache when she went in. By the time she left she had a severe bullet wound and, in addition, a suit for medical malpractice because of the negligent way her injury was treated. It all came about when a convicted criminal with a long record for violence and a habit of escaping from wherever he was confined complained that he too had a toothache. He was taken to the city hospital for dental treatment. Once there he showed a greater interest in going to the lavatory where a girl friend had previously stashed a revolver than in his dental problems. The prisoner came out shooting. He killed a guard and severely wounded Mrs. Nelson. A jury awarded Mrs. Nelson a total of $150,000. This was not merely a failure to provide police service, but a plain case of incompetent management of a dangerous criminal.

Out of Town, Out of Mind

Municipal mischief comes in all kinds of packages. There is black comedy as well as gold in suits against cities for police activity. Here is one rather incredible example.

A visitor from out of town was window shopping on Fifth Avenue in New York City one fine spring day some years ago. Suddenly, two large men appeared next to him, one on either side, and grabbed him. From this point on, the

story varies depending upon who tells the tale. According to
the out-of-towner's side, it appears that both men started to
beat him unmercifully, and the bystanders, after the fashion
of New Yorkers, ignored his cries for help while he was
dragged across the sidewalk and tossed into a wagon. The
two men tell a quite different version. They were New York
City detectives. A flyer described a man closely resembling
the out-of-towner as "armed and dangerous; approach with
caution," and noted that he had a phalange missing from his
left index finger. The detectives approached the visitor, identified themselves, and, they said, politely requested permission to inspect his left hand. Whereupon, they said,
the man violently attacked them and shouted, "All cops
are —————, —————, —————, and —————," a
completely uncensored thesaurus of police-directed insult.
By sheer coincidence, a police patrol wagon was passing by
and the driver, seeing the struggle, stopped to offer the
detectives transportation for the out-of-towner.

Both versions agree that when the patrol wagon unloaded
its cargo at the station house the out-of-towner emerged
struggling to free himself and shouted that he was being
beaten and kidnapped by a couple of brutes. By another
sheer coincidence, a police surgeon was leaving the station
house at that very moment. Seeing the commotion and hearing the screams, he winked at the desk sergeant and twirled
his finger at his temple. To the desk sergeant that gesture
meant a considered medical diagnosis of violent insanity,
and having no desire to turn his precinct into a loony bin,
he ordered two patrolmen to load the prisoner back into the
paddy wagon and deliver him to the city's Bellevue Psycho
Pavilion. When they arrived at Bellevue the out-of-towner
told the admitting physician his version of what had happened with considerable heat, while the patrolmen whispered
the police surgeon's "diagnosis" in the physician's ear. Those
were the days before tranquilizers, so the young psychiatrist

in training quickly had the man put in a strait jacket and gravely recorded the admitting diagnosis, "Paranoia, Manic, Possibly Suicidal." The out-of-towner went into the "tank." He might have stayed there a long time, but he had a surprising stroke of good fortune—Lord knows he was entitled to one. The evening before his adventure with the police, the out-of-towner struck up an acquaintance with a young woman in his hotel cocktail lounge and asked her out to dinner the next day. When he did not show up, the young lady, instead of coming to the normal conclusion that she had been stood up, waited more than an hour, checked with the desk clerk, and discovered that his key was in the box although he had not been seen all day. She persisted and had his room and the room maid checked out and discovered that he had not been in all night. With all the vigor of an innocent, the young lady pursued her investigation and traced the out-of-towner through the Missing Persons Bureau all the way to the loony bin at Bellevue. She retained a lawyer and rescued her friend from a durance viler than vile.

The suit by the visitor against New York City, the cops, the admitting physician, the casual police surgeon, and the desk sergeant for assault, false imprisonment, and medical malpractice seemed merely a minor prologue. And in those days before the Civil Rights Act a jury, bemused by a smart city lawyer, was led to find the events more diverting than damaging and returned a comparatively small verdict in the complainant's favor—awarding him only $5,000 in damages for an adventure he would have gladly paid far more to avoid. A better plaintiff lawyer would have waived a jury and obtained a better result from a judge, who is trained to keep his sense of fun out of the case.

So when can you sue for police failure? There is simply no clear rule. But there are categories of liability and nonliability—and they are changing. As we saw earlier, a municipality has a duty to provide police protection for the entire community. In order to fulfill that duty, city and police officials are entitled to assign personnel on a discretionary basis. In other words, they must decide how, when, and where to assign cops to best meet the needs of the entire community. If they fail to provide adequate police protection because they have misassigned personnel, it is the entire community that is affected, rather than the individual. Consequently, an individual who is also injured by such failure is *not* entitled to sue. For example, if too many police are assigned to area A, and you are injured in area B, you do not have the right to sue for lack of adequate police protection.

However, if you suffer injury as a result of circumstances that are not part of ordinary police procedure, you *are* entitled to sue. For example, if a city cop shoots you because he has not been properly trained in the use of firearms, the city is liable. If the police undertake the protection of one individual or put a criminal in a position to hurt a citizen or use a citizen as a shield or an informer or do anything that adds to the hazards of life—whether by police mischief or misconduct—the city is liable to suit. And, of course, if the city goes into business—running a railroad or some form of public transportation or operating an amusement park—it is bound to provide proper police security.

Educational Malpractice

A young man sued for damages against a local board of education because careless psychological testing when he entered kindergarten had placed him in special classes for the retarded, and he was treated and educated as a mongoloid up to age eighteen. It was then discovered that his intelligence was normal, that he was not mongoloid, and that he merely suffered from a speech defect. The treatment he had received actually suppressed his mind, retarded his development, and severely damaged his life.

When we consider how many children with speech, visual, and hearing defects have been treated as subnormal by careless school authorities, it seems obvious that the courthouse door has been opened wide to a multitude of suits for a new kind of claim—educational malpractice. This is a developing area of the law all over the nation, and a variety of actions are pending in the courts. Some of these cases are based on general law, and others are based on state constitutions and statutes that legally obligate municipalities to provide for the education of children. It is too early to tell what rules of law will develop by legislation and court decision.

However, if your child's life is marred by miseducation, a law suit should be considered. Recently, New York's highest court rejected the concept of educational malpractice as "against public policy," saying that educational matters must be left to school authorities. The decision is narrow and might not hold in other states. Suits under federal aid-to-education laws are independent of such litigation. These actions can help parents get proper education for exceptional (very bright or very backward) children. (See chapter VI for a detailed discussion of these suits.)

Choose a Partner

Suppose you are run down by an uninsured motorist who swerves suddenly and unskillfully to avoid a pothole. Obviously, the principal miscreant, who caused your misery, is the motorist. But the city, too, is involved, although only to a slight degree—it is not supposed to have potholed streets. Legally, the degree to which the city is at fault makes no difference as far as you are concerned. Even if the city's contribution is only 1 percent, and the motorist's is 99 percent, both are liable to the full extent of your damages. In many states these joint tort-feasors (another Norman-French term) are assessed their proper measure of liability between themselves, but each is fully liable as far as the injured party is concerned. So, provide the motorist with a rich partner. Sue both the city and the motorist and collect your damages from the city.

A taxicab stops far from the curb, and the alighting passenger steps into a hole in the street and is badly hurt. Both the taxicab operator—who carries the minimum required insurance—and the city are liable. A jury might tend to put most, but not all, of the blame on the taxi operator, but as long as the city is partly responsible, it is responsible for *all* the damages.

The following case is an interesting example of how this rule works. At 2 P.M. on a weekday, a tremendous gas explosion tore apart a multi-story building on Park Row in the center of downtown New York City—opposite City Hall. A blaze shot through the building, and within minutes the walls, floors, and ceilings collapsed into rubble. Twelve people were killed, and scores were badly hurt. A restaurant, a bar, stores, and shops vanished in a pile of debris. More than forty separate suits, claiming multi-million dollar damages, were brought against the owner of the building, the owner of the restaurant that had hired a plumber to install a new gas line, the public utility that supplied gas, and the city.

The reason all these defendants were sued illustrates the importance of hiring intelligent, creative lawyers. It is also a good example of the rule described above: even if you are only slightly at fault for an accident, you are wholly responsible to the injured person. In this case, the investigation showed that the restaurant was expanding from the ground floor to the second floor and needed a new gas line connection from the main gas line. It hired an out-of-town plumber who was not licensed in New York City and was not familiar with either the city regulations or the city gas line system. Before the utility would permit a new tap into its main line, it required an official certificate from a city inspector.

The blame seemed to fall on the restaurant owner who planned the gas line and hired the unlicensed out-of-town plumber instead of a knowledgeable city plumber, for reasons that can be imagined. And the plumber seemed equally at fault. The owner of the building, who had nothing to do with the events, was a corporation with no assets except the vanished building. The restaurant owner also was a corporation, who, together with its officers, had no assets and did not even bother to defend the multi-million dollar law suits. The plumber was a plain working man with nothing to put out. So the problem was to find a partner with money for these defendants. The lawyers found two solvent partners, the utility company and the city, and tied them neatly into the event. Here is what they proved.

The plumber made a defective connection to the main gas line from the basement of the building. He was pressured to get the job done quickly so that the restaurant could open for business after the weekend.

The city inspector apparently did not make the full inspection needed; he said that he did not know that there was anything other than a line to a meter included. He issued a certificate certifying that the gas pipe in question "conforms to the rules and regulations" of the city, even though it did nothing of the sort. Armed with this certificate, the restaurant applied to the utility company to have the gas turned on from the main line. The utility said it would come down and turn the gas on after the weekend. With that assurance, the restaurant owner got somebody else to turn on the gas. The odor of leaking gas led to an attempt to discover its origin: a small spark, an instant explosion, and the final disaster. After a series of hearings, appeals, and a new trial, the jury assigned the following percentages of responsibility for the accident to the various defendants: the defunct and defaulting restaurant, which did not even bother to defend the suit, was 80 percent to blame; the plumber was 12 percent at fault; the utility company was 4 percent to blame; and the city was 4 percent to blame.

However, as we have seen, anyone even partially responsible for an accident is totally liable as far as the injured person is concerned. The jury's allocation of responsibility only means that the defendant forced to pay the entire judgment can recover damages from the other defendants to the extent of their share of responsibility. Thus the city (or the utility) pays the entire multi-million dollar judgment and can recover 4 percent from the utility (or vice versa). And unless the city (or utility) has discovered how to get blood out of a stone, as the saying goes, that is the end of the game.

Moral: find a solvent defendant—no matter how slight his fault—when the principal wrongdoer is broke and judgment proof. And the city might well be that solvent defendant.

Contributory Negligence— Comparative Negligence

Until recently, if a person's conduct contributed in the slightest degree to the accident that caused his injury, he totally forfeited any right to sue. For example, if a person crossed in the middle of a city street and was knocked down by a speeding car, he was out of luck. He was, in legal language, contributorily negligent. Now, either by statute or judicial decision, the draconic rule of contributory negligence has been abolished in many states, and the more rational rule of comparative negligence has been substituted. An injured person can sue, even if the accident was partly his or her fault. The recovery against the defendant reflects the degree to which each the plaintiff and the defendant was at fault. This usually works to the advantage of the injured person.

For example, one night a young lad stepped over a low barrier in a city park and walked into the bushes to relieve himself. The darkness hid the fact that there was an unguarded twenty-foot drop to a lower level of the park behind the bush. The lad walked into a void, and dropped to the area below, breaking one arm, one leg, and a few ribs. Under the old contributory negligence rule, he would be out of luck. Under the new comparative negligence rule, the jury would decide to what degree the boy and the city were at fault and award the boy damages accordingly. Curiously, the boy's parents felt that the accident was his own fault and that there was something sinful about his having gone into the bushes in response to nature's call. They had to be nudged into bringing suit against the city involved.

IN SUMMARY

Do not assume that because you did something wrong, you are the only one to blame. Perhaps if you had not been speeding you would have seen the pothole in the road and avoided it. But then again, if the city had fixed the street, the pothole would not have been there. So serve a notice of claim and sue the city. You are partly to blame, but so is the city. And the jury will determine the percentage of your negligence and reduce the verdict accordingly.

Claiming and Suing Schedule

1. Get all the facts on paper. Do not rely on memory. Get names and addresses of witnesses. Photograph conditions before they change.
2. Prepare and serve a notice of claim.
3. Submit to required physical and oral examination. Make sure you are prepared for it.
4. Sue in time. Do not wait longer than necessary. And do

not start too soon. The city is usually entitled to thirty days after a claim before it can be sued.

5. A lawyer, a proper lawyer, is the best assurance of success. The sooner you retain a lawyer, the sooner he can get to work, investigating and getting written witness statements before witnesses are interviewed by the defendant.

6. A good settlement is better than the risk of a trial. But do not get shoved into a small settlement if it does not sound right. Ninety percent of the cases against municipalities are settled out of court.

7. If you go to trial and win, do not be surprised if the city appeals the decision. Often this is used as a sort of prolonged settlement process. But sometimes there are questions of principle that the city wants to settle.

Instituting a Suit

There is a wise adage; a lawyer who represents himself in a lawsuit has a fool for a client. A non-lawyer who tries to represent himself in a municipal lawsuit is in even worse shape. Most municipal suits are quite complex, and you will do yourself and your case a disservice if you attempt to litigate without an attorney. And since most of these cases can be handled on a contingency basis, legal assistance will present little or no financial hardship for you.

Because trial procedures are fairly complex and require a battery of special forms, it is impossible to cover the subject in great detail. However, it is useful to know what to expect in the most general way, and the following outline is offered for that purpose. And if you still insist on being your own litigator, it may help persuade you to hire a lawyer.

I. Prepare a summons and complaint. The summons is a printed form that you can buy in most stationery stores. The complaint is a more formal document.

II. The complaint must contain several items.

    A. The name of the Court where your suit is brought, as, "County Court, Wobble County."

    B. The title of the action, as

"John Jones,

Plaintiff

vs.

City of Blank,

Defendant.

    C. A statement describing the suit. For example: "Plaintiff for his cause of action against defendant alleges:

    1. Plaintiff, while riding a bicycle on Flint Street, City of Blank on January 2, 1979, was run down by a truck owned by defendant and operated by one of its employees in a grossly negligent manner.

    2. Plaintiff was rendered sick, sore, lame, and disabled by such acts of defendant and its employee.

    3. Plaintiff duly served an appropriate notice of claim on defendant on January 15, 1979.

    4. More than thirty days have elapsed since the said service of said notice of claim on defendant, and defendant has refused and failed to adjust such claim. Wherefore, plaintiff demands judgment against defendant in the sum of Fifty Thousand Dollars together with the costs of this action.

Dated: March 30, 1979

John Jones, Plaintiff

28 Misery Lane

City of Blank, Ind."

III. The city then serves an answer which, because cities always feel totally blameless, will consist of a general denial, "Defendant denies each and every allegation set forth in the complaint." It then goes on to ask that the "complaint be dismissed." At the same time, the city will probably ask for a bill of particulars; that is, every possible detail about the complaint—what happened; where it happened; when it happened; how it happened; and any other pertinent details.

IV. You must comply with the demand for particulars as completely as possible. You cannot use any particulars that are omitted at the trial.

V. The city will probably demand that you appear for an examination. You may already have done so when you served your notice of claim, but the city can require a second examination. You will be required to submit to a physical examination by a doctor, who will determine the extent and nature of your physical injuries. You will also be questioned about the details of your accident, and your statements and answers will be taken under oath. Before you appear for such an examination, figure out just what you are going to say, including when to cry "ouch" when the doctor tests you. This is not the time to act brave; if it hurts, let the doctor know. The oral examination is no simple matter. It takes training to handle yourself properly. You have to know which questions you do not have to answer, and you have to know what kinds of answers can ruin your case. Your testimony during this examination is taken down by a stenographer and can be read during the actual trial.

VI. You can ask to examine the driver of the city truck and take his testimony under oath at your own expense. You can also write out a series of questions, called *interrogatories,* which he has to answer, and you can use this information at your trial.

VII. Then, you must put your case on the court *calendar* by filing your complaint and paying a filing fee. In general, if your claim is over $10,000 the case goes to the highest court of original jurisdiction. In New York, for example, this would be the supreme court. If your claim is under $10,000 the case will be tried in an intermediate court, possibly civil court. The names of the various courts may differ from one municipality to another. Therefore, your best course of action is to visit the office of the court clerk and ask where and how you must go about filing.

VIII. Eventually, you will be reached for a *pretrial* conference. Generally, you are notified of this by the court. But in some large cities, you must find out when your case is on the calendar by calling or visiting the court clerk's office from time to time.

IX. At your pretrial conference, the judge will probably propose a settlement. If he does, take it and hope that he can convince the city to accept it. Otherwise you will have to wait for a trial and go through the misery of watching your position on the calendar, hanging around the court, looking for witnesses, subjecting yourself to cross-examination, and cross-examining the city's witnesses. It is not easy.

X. You might even win a verdict. If you do, you have to *enter a judgment,* that is, put the verdict in a written, formal document. You cannot do this by yourself. You will need the help of a court clerk who might take pity on you and give you aid and comfort.

XI. Serve the judgment on the city's lawyer. Then, be prepared for a long wait. You will probably have to badger the city lawyer and the city treasurer until you finally get paid.

All of this is oversimplified; it is actually far more complicated. There are pitfalls all along the way. Court proceedings, except in small claims court, are technical and absurdly complicated. There are form books in law libraries that contain forms for each of the various steps in a law suit—typical complaints, answers, bills of particulars, interrogatories, judgments, motions, petitions, and others. But even with the aid of such forms, it takes special skill to know how to use these tools. There is no substitute for skilled preparation for testifying, presenting evidence, cross-examining, or the other elements of a law suit. A non-lawyer is bound to slip up somewhere along the path.

Now really, wouldn't it make more sense to retain a lawyer on a contingency fee basis and leave the driving to him?

Small claims court is another matter. Generally, you can bring suit in small claims court if your claim is under $1,000. All major cities and many small localities have small claims courts. There, you buy a short-form complaint or a summons with a complaint endorsed on it, which the clerk mails to the defendant city. The date of trial is set. The proceeding is informal, almost conversational. The city sends its youngest lawyer, and the judge badgers him into a settlement—if there is merit to your complaint. Then you go through the process of collecting it, usually in a simplified manner.

CHAPTER IV

Righting Civil Wrongs

PERHAPS THE MOST dramatic change in the law during the sixties—a period of vast legal change—was the revival of the long dormant Ku Klux Klan Act of 1871. That act was designed to protect freed Negroes and federal agents in the conquered South from local government officials who had recovered from defeat and were intent on restoring the social and legal conditions of prewar times. Because that federal law's impact on municipal government is so pervasive, it is worth setting it forth:

> Every person who, under color of any statute, ordinance, regulation, custom or usage, of any state or territory, subjects or causes to be subjected, any citizen of the United States or other person within the jurisdiction thereof to the deprivation of any rights, privileges or immunities, secured by the Constitution and laws shall be liable to the party injured in an action at law, suit in equity or other proceeding for redress.

On its face, the sweep of the law is vast. Whatever local government officials do, they do "under color" of a "statute," or a local "ordinance," or a "regulation," or by virtue of a "custom or usage." And the "rights, privileges and immunities," which are secured by the Constitution and laws, are all the basic, protected aspects of civil rule that make life worth living.

Despite the breadth of its terms, federal courts originally interpreted the act practically out of the statute books. During the first ninety years of the act's existence only twenty-one cases were brought under its provisions, and all were rejected on one ground or another. In 1909, for example, a Georgia city police chief, under the false impression that a woman had spanked a relative's child, called the woman out of her house, publicly lashed her with a horsewhip, and put her in jail without charges. Unable to get relief from the local law enforcement authorities, she sued in the federal court. Her claim was rejected.

In 1961, all that changed. The United States Supreme Court awakened the act from its ninety-year sleep and gave it new life. Since then, as 42 United States Code (U.S.C.) 1983, it has been broadly interpreted by the courts and developed into the liveliest one-sentence statute on the books. These actions, commonly known as 1983 suits, have become the principal means of curbing local governments and local bureaucrats and righting the wrongs they have inflicted. In addition, the Federal Civil Rights Law has been amended recently to provide for the payment of plaintiff's counsel fees by the offending municipality and local officer. This has opened up a whole new variety of suits against cities in the federal courts. You do not have to be a black, a Hispanic, a Chicano, or a woman to sue for civil rights. The game is wide open; anyone can play. And the kinds of civil rights that can be violated and sued for keeps growing.

Definition of a 1983 Suit

A 1983 civil rights suit can be brought whenever a person is deprived of his rights under the Constitution. Equality of treatment under the law and due process are basic rights in our society, as is protection against cruel and unusual punishment, and discrimination on the grounds of race, creed, color, and gender. The terms are brief, but they can cover such a wide area of wrongs by cities and other local governments and government agencies that they defy cataloguing. The cases described in this chapter were chosen to illustrate the kinds of oppressive or unfair treatment for which 1983 offers protection. If the city has done you wrong in some unusual or special way, if it has denied to you what it has granted others or enforced laws against you that it does not enforce against others, the chances are that you have a 1983 case against a local government. There are lawyers who specialize in civil rights suits, and since they know that their fee, at a decent scale, is guaranteed to be assessed against the city if they succeed by trial or settlement, they will take your case for no fee at all or a very small initial fee.

Choice of Forum

1983 actions can be brought in state courts as well as in federal courts. Federal courts were originally made available for 1983 actions because the law was enacted in 1871 when it seemed unlikely that state courts, particularly in the defeated and angry South, could be expected to enforce that law. Although particular circumstances might dictate a state court 1983 suit, leave that decision to your lawyer. In general, in order to sue in federal court there must be diversity of citizenship. This simply means that the plaintiff and the defendant must be citizens of different states. 1983 suits are an exception to this rule, since such actions enforce a federally created right. And a set of circumstances that ordinarily would result in a lawsuit in state or local courts might also permit a 1983 suit in the federal courts.

Federal courts are the preferred forum for a variety of reasons. As a general rule, they are more efficient; they provide a better means of obtaining evidence through pretrial proceedings. On the whole they are more "correct"; there is less of the hurly-burly one often meets in state and local courts, particularly in the large urban centers. There are advantages in opting for a 1983 federal suit instead of an ordinary state court tort action against a municipality or local official in cases where either forum would be appropriate. The government immunity doctrine and notice of claim laws do not operate in 1983 suits, nor do laws limiting the amount of recovery. So, if a case brought as a tort case in the state court is barred or subject to limited recovery, recourse to a 1983 action might be the only real alternative.

We have already noted two lawsuits brought in state courts, which today could be instituted in federal courts under 1983; the out-of-towner who landed in Bellevue Psycho, and the two drunks left to dry out in an abandoned golf course. There would be several advantages in opting for a 1983 action in the latter case. The injury to the two drunks was directly attributable to a municipal police policy, so the city itself would be liable. Therefore, the plaintiffs could add their legal fees and costs to the amount recovered from the city. In the former case, the out-of-towner could bring a federal 1983 action against the two detectives and the desk sergeant, and under a New York statute the city would have to pay any damages and counsel fees awarded against the cops. And in both cases, the notice of claim laws would not apply.

1983 Municipal Indemnification

There is a special angle to 1983 actions. Damages can be recovered against the municipality for the misconduct of its officials only if the injuries were inflicted by reason of municipal policy or an accepted custom. Otherwise, only the individual public officials would be liable. However, in several states, New York for example, all local government officials are indemnified by the municipality if damages are assessed against them individually in 1983 cases—so the local government actually pays, not the employee. Similar indemnification laws have been enacted in Massachusetts, Connecticut, New Hampshire, and Illinois. This trend is spreading across the country as state and local officials are hit with judgments in 1983 cases. In some localities officials are being indemnified even in the absence of a law compelling it.

Some Examples of 1983 Cases

A high school boy in Pulaski, expelled for kissing a girl and exclaiming, "what a drag," when told by a teacher to stop, brought a 1983 suit in the federal court against the school board and the teacher. He was awarded damages of one dollar, and the court ordered that he be reinstated on the ground that the refusal of the school board to allow him to cross-examine the accusing teacher was a denial of his constitutional right of due process. His attorney, of course, can now claim counsel fees from the school board.

Do not assume that because you are a law-abiding citizen you will not have occasion to use 1983. Mistaken identity is far more common than is generally recognized, and mistaken apprehension is even more common. Things are often not what they seem to be. And the public official syndrome—the persistence of error—is a complicating factor. The following case is a classic example.

A health food maven bought a mixture of sage leaves and chopped up hard-boiled eggs, guaranteed to put hair on his chest and endow him with a potency beyond his wildest dreams. As he was carrying home this cellophane bag full of elixir of youth, he was stopped by an undercover narcotics cop, who mistook him for somebody else. Noticing the cellophane bag, the cop asked him if he was selling hashish. The health food maven, who would not know hashish from halibut, said no, he had sage leaves and chopped egg. The cop, assuming that he had discovered a new code expression for high-grade hash, offered him ten dollars for his package. The health food maven, who had just paid $1.25 for the stuff, told the cop he could get it down the street for $1.25. The cop would not be put off and pressed a ten dollar bill on the somewhat bewildered citizen and finally induced him to part with the stuff. As soon as the man handed it over, the cop revealed his identity, placed him under arrest, and marched him off to the station house. He was charged with two counts: possession of approximately ten ounces of a controlled substance (hashish), and sale of approximately ten ounces of a controlled substance (hashish). Both are Class A misdemeanors. It took the bewildered health food maven a week to raise the $500 bail set by the committing magistrate. During that time he was in the company of assorted murderers, rapists, and arsonists in the city prison. An inexperienced volunteer lawyer was the first person naive enough to believe the completely truthful tale. The lawyer pressured the prosecutor's office to make a chemical analysis of the hashish. To the prosecutor's astonishment it turned out to be sage leaves and hard-boiled egg. And the volunteer lawyer had a nice big 1983 suit against the cop and the city.

Professors, who are among the world's most timid souls outside the classroom, have found strong support in Section 1983. A few years ago, a professor at Brooklyn College, a branch of the New York City government, was preparing a study of political terrorism in European countries as part of his specialty, psychopolitics. He asked the Central Intelligence Agency for some background information before going abroad to collect material. The CIA asked him to get in touch with their staff on his return to discuss his findings. The professor did so in a fifteen-minute telephone call to a CIA official. A faculty committee construed his actions as amounting to "covert intelligence gathering," which violated academic integrity and reflected adversely on the college. The committee's recommendation that the professor be brought up on charges was not accepted by the college authorities, but he was nevertheless denied tenure. Recently, a federal district court jury, after a ten week trial, awarded the professor $580,000 in damages, plus $433,000 in counsel fees, plus $66,000 for costs of the suit.

In the famous *Bakke* case, which involved so-called reverse discrimination—a black student was accepted to a state medical school over a white candidate—the successful plaintiff's lawyer has billed the state $437,295 for his services.

Consider how Tammie Gilfin's parents made a federal case out of interference with her athletic interests. Tammie, to quote the court's opinion, was "a female junior in good academic standing" in Southeast High, Wichita, Kansas, who "enjoys long distance running and has a particularly keen desire to be" on the "cross-country team which has traditionally consisted solely of males." The Southeast High coach, a gallant fellow, gave Tammie the green light to join the boys on the team, but then "Tammie was informed that she could not participate on the boys' team because of a rule of the Kansas State High School Activities Association prohibiting participation by girls on boys' interscholastic athletic teams."

Tammie, asserting that her rights guaranteed by the equal protection clause of the Fourteenth Amendment to the United States Constitution had been violated, brought suit against all who would separate her from the boys. The United States District Court for the District of Kansas, in a solemn and learned opinion, which runs twenty double-column pages, gave judgment to Tammie and ordered the Kansas State High School Activities Association to forswear their male chauvinism, accept the Southeast High team with Tammie as a member, and, in addition, pay Tammie's lawyer a counsel fee and costs.

And, on the basis of the precedent laid down in Tammie's case, Jo Anne Carries of Wartsburg High in Tennessee won the right to try out for the baseball team. Congress, not to be upstaged by the federal judiciary, amended the Act to Incorporate Little League Baseball. They deleted the words "boys" and "manhood" from the federal charter which that Act granted, and substituted "young people," all of which, said Congress, was "to allow girls to participate on an equal basis with boys."

The Federal Court of Appeals in California recently sustained a woman's 1983 suit against a county board of supervisors. County officials had illegally shipped her mentally ill child back to Germany where he was born, without notifying the mother. The county seemed to feel that Germany, rather than its own institutions, should have the burden of caring for the child, who suffered from severe childhood schizophrenia.

The notion that a police officer may shoot a person who is running from the scene of a crime he has or appears to have committed simply is not true. And if a police officer shoots and kills or injures a person under such circumstances, the shooting must be justified by proving that the fleeing person was violent or was reasonably suspected of having committed a felony. Furthermore, the officer must be able to prove that all other means of apprehending him had failed. So, when city police came upon a boy climbing out of a window of a closed gas station, they ordered the child to halt. When he failed to obey the command, he was shot and killed. The city was held liable in a 1983 suit because city rules permitted such action by the police in such circumstances.

Apparently, the Soviet Union is not the only place where confinement to psychiatric institutions is used as a means of punishment. That seems to have been the practice with persons confined in prisons who act up. *One Flew Over the Cuckoo's Nest,* by Ken Kesey, described such a method of dealing with unruly or disobedient individuals. The federal courts and 1983 are available to persons so treated in municipal institutions, and the courts will give prompt relief and impose damage awards upon the staff and municipality involved.

Recently, in a 1983 suit, a federal court in New Jersey held that mental patients in a government-run hospital were entitled to refuse drug treatment in non-emergency cases. Written consent to such treatment was held necessary, and patients were also entitled to the services of a *patient advocate* who could be a lawyer, social worker, psychologist, or qualified nurse.

A municipal stadium was rented for a rock concert in Des Moines, Iowa. The city fathers arranged for several dozen police officers, complete with uniform and side arms, to work during off-duty hours at the rock concert. The youngsters entering the stadium were subjected to a body search and shakedown of packages and pocketbooks. The federal court put a stop to the practice. Warrantless searches, said the court, violates the Constitution, and its victims and potential victims are entitled to relief. The court said:

> IT IS THEREFORE ORDERED that the defendant commissioner and manager of Veterans Memorial Auditorium are henceforth permanently enjoined from subjecting plaintiff and the members of the class they represent, to unconstitutional searches of their person, purses, parcels, clothing and other personal effects as a condition for entry to rock concerts at Veterans Memorial Auditorium.

And the court further ordered a hearing on the amount of counsel fees to be awarded.

More 1983 Cases

There is almost a limitless variety of 1983 actions against cities and counties. A young boy running from a vacant abandoned house, where he and a friend had been playing, was shot dead by a city policeman who had a history of violent and careless conduct. The city was successfully sued by the parents.

A city mandated an unpaid maternity leave commencing four months after the onset of pregnancy and ending four months after the termination of pregnancy. The city was successfully sued for violation of civil rights.

When a city airport concession was compelled by the city to remove copies of *Penthouse* magazine from its newsstand, the publishers were entitled to sue under 1983.

Teachers denied reappointment because they sent their own children to private schools recovered judgment against the city under 1983.

A municipal hospital refused to perform elective abortions and was successfully sued under the Civil Rights Act.

A city employee who was fired for joining a union recovered a judgment under 1983.

When a city housing inspector and a policeman, under the false impression that a building had been condemned and was unlawfully occupied by squatters, crashed through the door to an apartment and demanded evidence of rent and paid utility bills, the occupant had a solid claim against the city under 1983.

A city was successfully sued under 1983 for failing to train its police properly in the handling of guns and in nonviolent law enforcement. The plaintiffs, although law violators, were permitted recovery for injuries sustained during their arrest.

In several different cases, students in city schools recovered awards for the indignity suffered when they were strip searched by teachers looking for drugs and stolen property.

Medical neglect of detainees and prisoners in city facilities has resulted in substantial awards under 1983.

A county's deliberate denial of relocation benefits to families in the path of a federally supported local highway construction project were similarly entitled to separate damages in a 1983 suit.

The withholding of vested pension rights of a former county employee was the basis of a 1983 suit for damages.

A city employee, who was fired for circulating a petition protesting fire department promotion policies, recovered damages for denial of constitutional rights.

When a city operates a water supply system or a gas and electric power system, it cannot cut off the service to an individual without a hearing. If it does, it subjects itself to a 1983 suit for a denial of due process. A recent suit against a city utility, which cut off service without a due process hearing, was successful.

A city policeman, who was fired because he refused to answer questions about his out-of-wedlock sexual adventure with an eighteen-year-old girl successfully sued for reinstatement and damages. A federal court declared that the questioning was an unconstitutional invasion of his private life.

Three young children were riding in a car driven by their uncle on a busy limited-access highway one evening. City police stopped the car, arrested the uncle for speeding, and took him to the station house in their patrol car. The uncle begged the cops to bring the children along, or at least take them to a phone so they could call their parents. The cops turned the request down and abandoned the kids in their uncle's car. The children waited patiently for help. None came. Finally, in the pitch dark, terrified out of their wits, they miraculously managed to get across eight traffic lanes of the speedway and wandered along until they were rescued by a stranger and taken home. All the kids were in a state of shock. One, an asthmatic, ended up in the hospital. A 1983 suit was upheld. The children and their parents got an award, and counsel fees were assessed against the city and the cops.

A cozy arrangement between a local bank and the city police provided a 1983 suit. The bank was anxious to collect on Mr. L's loan before his other creditors took action. They worked out a deal with the accommodating city officials: Mr. L. was arrested for nonpayment of a parking ticket and held in the station house cell. The bank employees then came around and told him that the bank had arranged to have him locked up and would arrange to keep him there unless he paid off his loan. This fancy form of debt collecting resulted in a successful 1983 suit against the city, the cops, and the bank.

Consider the case of a rather wiggly young woman who roamed around a somewhat sleazy area of the city wearing tight pants and waving to passing motorists. Two cops pulled her in for prostitution. But after a night in a station house lockup she was released when it became apparent that she was just a nice friendly girl without a blemish on her character or an evil notion on her mind. She thought she had a good civil rights suit against the city, but the federal court decided that the city was blameless because it had no established policy of locking up cheerful and legitimate young ladies. Furthermore, the cops were entitled to act on appearances since they could not really know what was on the lady's mind.

In a similar case, a New York City policeman was transporting a bevy of prostitutes to the lockup late one night. They had been picked up in a neighborhood commonly known among the cops as the East Side's Minnesota Strip— an area, like its raunchier namesake in Times Square, where prostitutes, supposedly refugees from the harsh farm life in the Midwest, gather to ply their trade in a fancy neighborhood. The cop's attention was drawn to a young blonde woman walking alone on Park Avenue who was identified by one of the captured prostitutes as someone who had "ripped me off in the Tombs [a city prison] last week." The cop stopped the car and chased the woman who, thinking she was being pursued by a mugger (the cop was in plainclothes), screamed "Police, help." The cop caught up with her, grabbed her by the hair, dragged her back to the car, and tossed her in among the other captives. The accusing prostitute then calmly announced that she had made a slight mistake; she had fingered a perfect stranger. The blonde turned out to be a lady of impeccable character. The cop's apologies to the outraged citizen were *not* gratefully accepted, and the result was one more 1983 suit against the city and the cop. Under New York law, the city is bound to protect its officers against the judgment for awarded damages.

In all of these, and in other similar cases, counsel fees are awarded against the offending municipalities and officials if you can prove your case. In granting counsel fees, the federal courts are no respecters of persons. In a recent 1983 case, the Virginia Supreme Court was ordered to pay a $100,000 counsel fee to a consumer protection organization. The agency had successfully sued the Virginia Supreme Court, and outlawed that court's rule prohibiting advertising by attorneys.

CHAPTER V

The Federal Factor

WHEN A LOCAL government applies for and accepts federal funds for its various activities it discovers that there are strings attached to the grants, which sometimes seem to make them hardly worth the trouble they generate. For example, a municipality that enjoys any federal grant or federally assisted program commits itself to provide the handicapped with access to all public buildings and facilities. Sidewalk cuts and building ramps to accommodate wheelchair citizens are fast becoming a familiar sight in our cities. When federal aid is granted, cities must also agree not to discriminate against the handicapped. Now that, of course, should not bother a municipality, but for the fact that the term handicapped includes narcotics addicts and alcoholics.

This circumstance has bothered the New York City Transit Authority, which operates a city-owned rapid transit system and bus lines with substantial federal aid for physical improvement and operation. Our country's almost 7½ million physically handicapped have probably been the most discriminated against group in recent times. They were not merely limited to riding "in the back of the bus," they could not get on the bus at all—even if it was city owned and operated. The physically handicapped citizens are only now becoming aware of their legal rights, and a new class of civil rights law remedies are being provided for the assertion and protection of those rights. Recently adopted federal rules require that every kind of public transportation receiving federal aid be made available to the physically handicapped. New York City's elaborate rapid transit system is almost totally inaccessible to most physically handicapped people who cannot navigate stairways. This contrasts with the London Underground, which has very few stairs and the Washington, D.C. system, which has more. Compliance with the federal rules will take many years and billions of dollars to accomplish. A maximum of thirty years is permitted for compliance. But progress is being made with the advent of *kneeling* buses, which accommodate the severely crippled and wheelchair occupants. Municipal surface transportation systems are now being forced to use these buses. There is considerable resistance to this whole movement; suits have even been brought by some cities to invalidate the law and the rules. But organizations of the physically handicapped can get both federal and state court aid in obtaining what the wheelchair victim regards as long overdue. Obviously, suits of this nature by individuals are not practical. But action is being taken by the growing organizations of the handicapped. Just such a suit is in the New York courts, and it will remain there for some time because the issues and possible remedies are very complex.

A city that accepts a federal grant for public works must agree to arrange its construction contracts so that at least 10 percent of the federal grant will go to minority enterprises— enterprises whose principal owner is black, Spanish-speaking, Eskimo, or Aleut.[1] Presumably, a group of Aleuts can form a

---

1. Aleuts (pronounced alley-oots) are a tiny ethnic minority who live in the Aleutian Islands off the coast of Alaska. How they can fit into the kind of massive construction operations typical of government contracts is one of the more intriguing mysteries of contemporary federal bureaucracy.

construction company in Chicago and demand an appropriate share of municipal construction work financed by federal grants. And the Aleuts do *not* have to prove that they employ Aleuts or, for that matter, any other minority. It is the *enterprise* that is preferred, not the employees of the enterprise. This, too, is pending before the courts.

State and local acceptance of federal grants for any purpose (and literally all states get federal funds for several purposes) imposes all kinds of special duties and requirements on local governments, particularly in regard to children's education. There are special provisions in federal statutes governing educational assistance for the handicapped, as well as for "children with specific learning disabilities." The latter category is a vast undefined area that includes the very common handicap of dyslexia, a reading disability ranging from moderate to severe and prevalent in very bright children of middle-class families. Handicapped children are entitled to special education at no cost, and these are rights that can be enforced by application to the federal Office of Education, to the federal courts, and even to the state courts. The United States Supreme Court decided recently that a Chinese child in a city school in Oregon was entitled to be taught in Chinese until she was able to manage English. In another case, a Federal district court compelled a school district to provide a sign-language interpretation for a deaf child.

By using federal funds for education, local school districts subject themselves to controls, rules and regulations that grant special rights to a variety of special groups. A single aspect of this—the right of exceptional children to exceptional treatment, including not only the exceptionally slow and retarded but also the exceptionally quick and intelligent —has been the subject of exhaustive comment and study by Jack B. Weinstein, a distinguished professor of law and an outstanding federal judge. The parent of a child with special problems has a right to sue for special educational assistance.

Regardless of the nature of the educational problem, you have a right to receive appropriate assistance from the city, town, or village school authorities.

Every state is required by federal law to provide a method for giving proper education aid to a handicapped child. Parents of such children can receive specific assistance in determining what is required of the local educational authority and how such requirement may be enforced by addressing an inquiry describing the particular situation to:

> United States Office of Education,
> Bureau of Education for the Handicapped,
> 400 Maryland Avenue, SW,
> Washington, D.C. 20202.

These are enforceable rights, and local school boards and state education agencies are required to provide special educational services at no cost to the parents, whether or not the parents have financial resources. If they are not granted, suit may be brought to enforce them. But, state and local school authorities are well aware of their obligations to handicapped children and usually will not risk the loss of federal funds by failing to obey the law. New York City, where most of these cases seem to occur, is confronted with lawsuits that can add $27,000,000 to its education for the handicapped expenditures.

CHAPTER VI

Reducing Property Taxes

GENERALLY, LOCAL GOVERNMENTS are supported largely, and in some cases almost exclusively, by real estate taxes. These taxes are based upon the assessed value of the property taxed. The owners of large real estate holdings almost automatically protest the assessments of their property as soon as they receive notice of the assessment. There is a separate and very busy section of the bar whose members devote themselves to what are called certiorari proceedings—reviewing assessments of real property. Small property owners—householders—generally accept increases in the assessed valuation of their property without complaint, assuming that complaint is hopeless. Actually this is not so. A protest of a tax assessment very often results in a reduction.

Grieving on Grievance Day

Each tax-assessing unit—city, county, town, village, or district—fixes a specific day or number of days following the completion of real property assessment for taxpayers' complaints. During this time, property owners can formally protest or appeal the assessment made on their property. This date is generally set by a local ordinance or regulation and is called grievance day, protest day, appeal day, or review day —the first name being the most common.

Grievance days vary from place to place with such diversity that no adequate or reliable table can be made that will be either accurate or current. For example, in New York State fifty-five different grievance days are fixed by the sixty-two cities, and a score or more are set for the various villages and counties. Some set a single day aside for grieving; others two, four, or five days; still others one, two, four, and even six weeks. And all are fixed at different times of the year.

Unless you file a protest against the assessment of your property on your local grievance day or days, you will not be able to get the assessment changed. To protect your right to challenge the assessment, find out the dates fixed for grievance day in your area. Visit the assessor's office and ask or demand to see the ordinance or regulation that fixes grievance day. And make sure you go early so that you can compare your assessment with assessments on other property.

Remember, if you do not file your protest and file it on time, you can not get action either from assessors or from the courts. In New York City, assessment books are open from February 1 to March 15. During that period taxpayers can formally protest and be heard by the Tax Commission. *Technical compliance with protest requirements is essential for the property owner to preserve his rights.*

Sophisticated small property owners can take care of the protest or grievance procedures themselves without retaining counsel. However, if, for example, a new housing subdivision is created and placed on the tax rolls, the individual property owners would be well-advised to join together and retain a tax certiorari lawyer to take all appropriate steps toward a reduction in assessments. By banding together the property owners can make it worthwhile for the lawyer to take the proceeding through the assessment agency and to the courts on a contingency basis, fixing his fee, usually 33⅓ percent, at a percentage of the taxes saved by the reduction of each year's assessment.

Assessment Protest

The property tax is a fixed rate applied to the assessed value of the property as generally determined by local government assessors. Essentially, a property owner can protest his assessment on two grounds: overvaluation and inequality. Overvaluation means that the property is worth less than the assessor says it is worth. Inequality means that the property is unequally assessed; it has been assessed at a higher percentage of its value than other similar property. Inequality arises out of a variety of circumstances. For example, in urban areas it is a common practice to assess private residences at a fraction of their true value, and to assess commercial and industrial property at either full value or something close to full value. The reasons for this are political and economic: homeowners vote in great numbers; corporations do not vote at all. Since election is the principal end sought by all non-appointed officials, a lower tax rate for homeowners is politically advantageous. From the economic standpoint, commerce and industry are generally better able to bear taxes than ordinary citizens. The system is similar to graded income taxes, which are designed to get more money from the rich than from those who are not rich.

Nationwide, private residences are assessed at an average of 30 percent of their real value. In certain suburban residential tax districts, all property is assessed at a uniform percentage of its real value so inequality does not apply; a tax rate of 5 percent on 50 percent valuation is exactly the same as 2½ percent on 100 percent valuation. But in many localities there is no uniformity of valuation. Within the residence class there are wide differences between the rate of value at which private houses are assessed, depending upon their age and the last date of purchase, regardless of their actual worth. In New York City private residences that have not changed ownership over the past forty or more years continue to be assessed every year at the value fixed for them when Fiorello H. La Guardia was mayor in the late thirties. Low assessments for residences and high assessments for commercial and industrial property were the practice in New York State for more than 200 years, despite a statute in effect during all that time that required every kind of property to be assessed at its *full value.* In 1975, when the state's highest court, in a decision that astonished the tax assessing officials, applied that statute according to its express language, the result was so potentially disruptive and threatening to middle- and lower-middle-class home owners that the court deferred the effective date of the decision by permitting the reassessment of property to be delayed for several years. The state legislature delayed it even further and for several years has been casting about for a way to undo what the court did.

To preserve the stability of the tax base that provides the major source of revenue for the local government, local taxing authorities have developed a variety of means to make it as difficult as possible to challenge assessments. In turn, taxpayer groups seek to overcome these roadblocks by obtaining state legislation simplifying the review and revision of assessments. Recently, in New York, as a result of court interpretation of a statute, judicial review of assessments for inequality became extremely simple and was practically guaranteed to result in reduction. This is how it worked. A state body made surveys to estimate the percentage of actual value that various local government assessors were using to assess properties. This was called the *equalization rate.* For example, an equalization rate of fifty for a particular tax district meant that the district assessed local property at only

50 percent of its actual value. The courts held that any tax-payer could have his assessment reduced by proving that his property was being assessed at a higher percentage of its real value than the percentage estimated by the state for local property. So all that a property owner had to do was establish the actual value of his property with the help of an experienced appraiser. If, for example, an expert appraiser valued your property at $10,000, and the property was locally assessed at $10,000, but the equalization rate was 50, that would prove your assessment should have been $5,000, and you would be entitled to have it reduced to that amount.

In New York City alone, this court decision resulted in 125,000 inequality petitions, and almost 30,000 were filed in an adjacent suburban county. Threatened with a potential liability for refunds of $2,700,000,000 in overpaid taxes, the city enacted a law to unsimplify the procedure by abolishing the use of the equalization rate in all pending and future review proceedings. This law is being challenged and will not be resolved until some time in the next few years.

In some states inequality claims are discouraged by a very simple device. If a property owner claims that his property is overassessed in relation to other similar properties, those properties are reassessed; he cannot demand a reduction in the assessment of his own property. In other states, appeals of local property assessments are heard by state administrative boards whose decisions are final and, for all practical purposes, beyond judicial review.

The task of evaluation of real estate is highly complex, and the complexity itself is a form of built-in taxation. Nevertheless, reduction of assessments is common in all taxing jurisdictions. And since the bases of valuation are the same no matter where the property is located, some general rules and practical suggestions for obtaining reductions can be made. Remember, it costs nothing to ask for a reduction of assessment on the local assessor level and on the local assessment review board level.

Overvaluation Assessment

As we have seen, strict overvaluation is not common, since assessment is almost always less than true value. You can prove overassessment by the testimony of an expert appraiser who will show the selling price of substantially identical property, the purchase price of the property in question if bought recently, the market value of the property, and finally, what, in his judgment, is a fair valuation. Opposing testimony or evidence may be submitted by the municipal assessor, and a determination will be made by an official assessment board. In most cases the determination will be subject to review by a court.

Inequality Assessment

Inequality is the most common form of overassessment because property is rarely assessed on an annual basis. Therefore, in a period of rising values, new assessments of new buildings are bound to be higher than unchanged assessments of older buildings. Houses do not depreciate like automobiles. A fifteen-year-old private dwelling will usually be worth as much, if not more, than a nearby newly built dwelling of the same size. Yet, it is often assessed at far less than the new and therefore newly assessed dwelling. Thus, on its face, inequality exists, regardless of whether the new building is assessed at less than its actual value. Although, commonly, inequality is not demonstrated by an isolated discrepancy of the sort mentioned. It is entirely possible in such circumstances to obtain a reduction of assessment at the local level, usually by agreeing to settle out of court. This is quite common and worth trying. It very often works. Generally, however, proof of inequality is required by a sampling of a number of similar dwellings.

The appendix contains a sample set of forms for correction of assessment at the administrative appeal level; that is, the Board of Assessment Appeal, or whatever local name it has. These forms are used in New York City. However, the kind of information requested is substantially the same as that generally requested by tax assessment review agencies. In fact, cities tend to copy one another's forms, ordinances, and regulations, so the forms in the appendix, both for private dwellings and large rental premises, are useful models.

The fact that your property is assessed at less than its actual sale value does not necessarily mean that you are not entitled to a reduction of assessment for local property tax purposes. As we have seen above, real estate, and especially private residential property, is commonly assessed for property tax purposes at less than its actual value. Fractional assessment, as it is called, it almost always the rule rather than the exception. It can range from 19 percent of true value to 40 percent, and rarely goes above 80 percent. And this is true even where the statutes require full value assessment. In localities that adhere to fractional assessment, you are entitled to a reduction of assessment on your home or other real property, with a consequent reduction of local property tax, if you can show that other property of the same class is generally assessed at a lower fraction of real value than yours is. Ask your local assessor how property is assessed in your area; if he has any conscience, he will tell you the truth. Check tax assessment rolls; they are public records and you are entitled to look at them. It is not really difficult to make out a case for inequality if it exists. It is only a matter of paying attention.

Once you have discovered inequality, file a protest (forms are generally provided by the assessor or the assessment review board) and detail the basis of your claim. You may be surprised to find that your appeal is successful. In states that permit court review a reduction may be more readily granted if you agree not to appeal the decision to the court. You also have the right under general law and more particularly under the various freedom of information acts (see chapter XI) to examine applications made by other property owners and check the assessors' determinations of these applications.

Real estate taxation is generally recognized as retrogressive, unbalanced, and irrational in many respects. But efforts to reform the assessment process have not shown any brilliant success. If all property is assessed and taxed at literally full value, homeowners who now enjoy a lower percentage of value assessments would find their taxes doubled, while industry and commerce taxes would be reduced. Such a solution is not only practically hazardous, but sociologically disruptive to the pattern of a community's life. Proposals have been made to classify different kinds fo property and apply either different assessment percentages or different tax rates to different categories. But this has turned out to be complicated and of limited value. Minnesota, for example, is struggling with no fewer than forty different classes and subgroups, and the proliferation continues as different kinds of occupants exert pressure for favorable treatment. And the more complex the subject becomes, the more varied and numerous are the opportunities for protest and possible tax reduction by the alert property owner.

IN SUMMARY

1. Find out when the local grievance day is.
2. Check the tax assessment rolls (before grievance day) for discrepancies between your assessment and your neighbor's or any other property similar to yours.

3. If your assessment is out of line and higher than comparable property, get a protest form, fill it out, and file it in the assessors' office on time. Do not wait for grievance day to get the form. Get it early and hold it until you are ready to use it.

4. Try to negotiate a reduction with the assessor. If that does not work, appeal to whatever assessment appeals board has been established.

5. Try to make a deal to settle before the appeals or review board.

Finally, if it seems worthwhile, find a tax certiorari lawyer willing to take your case on a contingency basis.

And, if you are one of a whole group of homeowners in a new subdivision, join hands with them, get a lawyer, and get him before the tax rolls are complete because you can be almost certain that you, as the new taxpayer, are going to have something to complain about.

CHAPTER VII

Eminent Domain

Property Seizure—History and Limits

To a nation steeped in the tradition of due process, constitutional protection against government incursion and invasion of rights, the manner in which private property is seized for public purposes is often shocking. If you have not personally experienced the exercise of what is called eminent domain, you cannot really understand what it feels like—the shock of discovering that your house is suddenly not yours, or that a chunk of your lawn or a portion of your porch belongs to a faceless bureaucracy. The courts, in their remote view of things, see it this way: the right to take property for public use—eminent domain—is a reserved right attached to every man's land and to his right to ownership. He holds his land subject to that right and cannot complain of injustice when it is lawfully exercised.

Private property can be taken by the government for *any* public purpose. Eminent domain, for such is its ancient and fancy title, is regarded as an inherent power of the sovereign state. The key words are *the sovereign;* in ancient times all land belonged to the king or sovereign. The sovereign could give land to a subject, but he could also take it back. One of the basic rights granted in the Fifth Amendment to the United States Constitution is the right to compensation: "nor shall private property be taken for public use, without just compensation." An equivalent provision can be found in the constitutions of the individual states. And the due process requirements of the Fourteenth Amendment bolster this right. However, such provisions are based on the unquestioned assumption that a government, even a republican form of government, has the power of the ancient king to take whatever private property it wants for the general good. The Constitution only guarantees that property so taken will be taken for a public purpose and will be paid for.

The meaning of public purpose has expanded so over the years that it is difficult to find a purpose that cannot be described or disguised as public. And the sovereign power of eminent domain can, and is, delegated to local governments of all kinds for all sorts of purposes. A few examples are housing and urban development, railroad and economic development, hotels, and art museums with air rights over them to sell to private apartment house developers in order to help support the museum. New "public" purposes are invented every year. In short, a consideration of the limits of eminent domain is less useful than an examination of how it happens to you.

How It Happens: Quick Taking and Notice

The *lawful exercise* of eminent domain ranges from notification of a pending court proceeding—usually too late to do anything about it—to what is candidly called *a quick taking* procedure. In the latter process, private property instantly becomes public property after a paper has been filed in a government office. Trades and industries have been radically and adversely affected by the use of eminent domain. In the exercise of sovereign power, businesses, particularly small businesses, have been obliterated. Only in recent years has there been some amelioration of the serious injustices that often accompanied the exercise of the condemnation power. Now, in New York and in some other states, the exercise of eminent domain must be preceded by a notice of a public hearing on the proposed project that requires the condemnation action. In all parts of the country, property owners must be formally notified that their property has been taken and they must be paid for the value of their property. However, there are limitations even upon this basic constitutional right of compensation.

How Much Do You Get?

As the courts have stated, the government pays only for property seized for its own use. It does not pay for what it takes *from* the owner. For example, since the government is not acquiring a business, but only the premises in which the business operates, it only pays for the bare value of the premises and the land on which it stands, even though that does not nearly compensate the owner for the loss of a going business. Under that doctrine the owner of a candy store, a liquor store, or a barber shop taken in condemnation gets nothing for the loss of the business and the goodwill built up over the years, which has enhanced the value of his establishment. If he rents the building, he is entitled at most to the value of the remainder of his lease, assuming, that is, that he has not signed the usual lease which provides for its automatic termination upon condemnation.[1] In that event, he gets nothing, and the landlord receives the full compensation. Under ordinary condemnation law such a businessman is not even reimbursed for the cost of moving his business to another location.

---

1. This is something to look out for when signing a lease. Usually, a landlord will let you strike out such a provision and doing so might save you a great deal if the city suddenly decides to condemn the building in which you are a tenant.

Federal statutes have forced local governments who take property for purposes and projects paid wholly or partly by federal grants to ease this standard condemnation law slightly. As a result, the serious deprivations imposed upon people whose property is taken in condemnation are gradually becoming less severe throughout the country.

What You Get Paid For

For the homeowner and small business operator to whom this book is addressed (large corporations know what to do in condemnation matters), there are certain general rules that are useful to know. For example, your local government is building a limited access highway and is taking a strip of your frontage in condemnation. You have the right to receive compensation for that part of your property. You might also be entitled to the total value of your house if part of it is taken. You also have the right to buy back the house as salvage and move it out of the way of the highway. If you are a tenant, you might be entitled to moving costs. An owner may be entitled to relocation benefits. If the property is business property, you might be entitled to the very substantial costs of relocating your business. The cost of moving a factory containing massive machinery can run into vast sums. In New York an amusement park with elaborate death-defying rides, carousels, machinery, booths, and other equipment was on property condemned by the city. The price tag for disassembling, moving, and reassembling the equipment ran well over $1½ million.

Beware the Friendly Negotiator

Local governments that condemn property employ negotiators to obtain property for as little as possible. They are generally smooth talkers who inspire confidence. Lest you think that government negotiators do not really care how much the government has to pay for your property, remember that it is their job to get the property cheaply. Studies show that property owners who settle with negotiators when their property is condemned get about 50 percent of the lowest estimate of the value of their property. When they are represented by competent counsel, they get as much as 200 percent of such an estimate.

In some states, New York for example, the condemning authority is obliged to pay the property owner 100 percent of the appraised value as determined by the government's own experts, and such payment is to be made without prejudice to the right of the property owner to claim additional money in a court proceeding. Despite this provision of law, local governments take advantage of the unwary by asking them to sign a receipt for the advance payment, which includes an express waiver of any further claims for any additional money. The government appraisal value is not necessarily the actual value. Commonly it is at most 60 percent of what a court will award for the property.

All of this emphasizes the need for a property owner to retain a competent condemnation lawyer to protect his interests. And it need not cost anything. In such circumstances, condemnation lawyers generally take such claims on a contingency basis. They are paid a percentage of what they recover over and above the advance payment or the offer of the negotiator.

The commonly accepted base rate of the contingency fee arrangement is around 5 percent of the total recovered. A recovery over the advance payment commands a different rate and is a matter of negotiation. The attorney usually will base it upon an estimate of the recovery made by his own expert appraiser. In any retainer agreement of this kind the property owner should make sure that the legal services include relocation benefits, moving expenses, and the right to acquire salvaged property such as a house or other structure that can be moved. Usually the condemnation lawyer will throw in such additional services at no additional charge.

Relocation Benefits: The Federal Factor

Relocation benefits and moving expense payments are new to the field of condemnation. Until Congress placed conditions on federal grants, which in turn obligated municipalities who received those grants to provide such benefits and payments, people who lived in the path of a highway or other public improvement were not much better off than if they were in the path of a cyclone; they got blown away in another sense. The only exception was when a large city, like New York or Boston, needed to take over an area outside its own limits for its water supply purposes. In that kind of situation, rural dominated state legislatures were glad to make the big city people "behave properly." In authorizing condemnation outside the city's borders, the legislature imposed generous awards to the rural folk affected. In rural New York, for example, anyone who could show that the place where they worked was taken by New York City for water supply purposes—its reservoirs are in rural areas a great distance from the city—received six months salary. A clergyman, whose congregation was depleted when his parishioners' property was condemned, also got a substantial award although his church was not even in the area taken by the city.

One of the important advantages to persons whose property is taken by a federally funded highway or other federally supported public works is the comparatively generous relocation benefits provided by or imposed by federal law. Although such benefits hardly compensate for the misery of being uprooted, until recent times and before Congress enacted the Uniform Relocation Benefits Act, businesses were

ruined and lives disrupted in the course of the usual municipal condemnation. Owners got the bare value of their land
and building, and in the case of factory and business premises, the depreciated value of machinery and equipment that
could not be removed without radical damage. Tenants generally received nothing because their leases usually did not
reserve any right to any part of a condemnation award.

The impact of federal involvement has been growing in
significance as more and more federal funds are provided for
local capital improvements. Industrial and commercial property owners and tenants are now entitled in federally aided
condemnation to the actual cost of moving their establishments, lock, stock, and barrel. Entire factories, plants, and
commercial establishments are now disassembled, moved to
new locations, and reassembled at the expense of the government. And a very large expense it can be!

Homeowners and residential tenants are also entitled to
relocation benefits. And federal authorities insist that property owners and tenants be treated fairly. But remember,
knowledge of the simple fact that you *may have* rights makes
a very big difference. Once you know that, go further and
find out what those relocation rights are.

In the case of the displaced homeowner, the benefits include the value of the land and the building and the difference between the compensation received and the cost of another similar home. If there was a mortgage on the home, the
homeowner is also entitled to the difference between the
mortgage interest rate and the rate he will have to pay for a
mortgage on his new house plus his moving expenses and all
the closing costs on the purchase of the new home.

Residential tenants compelled to move from the site of a
federally aided municipal project are entitled to social and
economic help. They must be assured of "decent, safe and
sanitary" replacement living quarters—a house or an apartment. Relocation benefits to residential tenants, up to a max-

imum of $4,000 in value, may include assistance toward providing a down payment on the purchase of a dwelling, or the differences between the old rent paid and the new rent required in the replacement dwelling. Additionally, the tenant must receive moving expenses—either actual or a fixed amount from $225 to $300 depending upon the number of rooms in the dwelling—plus a dislocation allowance of $200.

In a period when home construction costs are high, it might be worthwhile to retain the house and move it to another site. If the cost of moving it is greater than the government's award for the property, the government will make up the difference in the actual cost of moving plus the cost of acquiring and purchasing a new site. Another possibility is to take the award for the house and then negotiate with the municipality for the purchase of the house and move it yourself.

What to Do and When to Do It

1. When you get your first notice that your property is being taken by the city, do not panic. It is not going to happen immediately; you are not going to be tossed out of your home by Monday morning. There will be time to consider and think and discuss with your neighbors and fellow victims.

2. It is very likely that federal money is involved in the project for which your property is needed. If it is, you have less to worry about. Uncle Sam is usually more generous than either your state or your local government. Find out if there is federal involvement, and what federal agency it is. Write to the federal agency involved and get some of the multitude of regulations and bulletins they issue. They have lots of information about what you are in for and what you are entitled to.

3. Unless you are extremely knowledgeable or skilled in

this area, get a lawyer—one skilled in condemnation proceedings. Offer to pay him a percentage over the government's highest offer. Generally, in federally aided projects, the condemning authority pays its highest offer on demand, and you can go ahead with the money in hand and ask for more. Watch out for the friendly negotiator and do not sign anything that waives *any* of your rights.

4. Use the government's publications to check on whether you are getting a square deal.

5. Check up on your relocation rights. Even tenants are entitled to relocation benefits in many states, and you are *always* entitled to such benefits when federal funds are involved. There are all kinds of forms and pamphlets on relocation that you can get on demand in federally aided projects. Read them and ask the issuing agency to explain anything you do not understand.

CHAPTER VIII

Doing Business
with the City

There ought to be a death's head sign posted in municipal procurement offices:

> WARNING, dealing with the city may be hazardous to your business.

The Watchword Is Watch Out

Local governments spend literally billions of dollars on materials, services, equipment, and construction. They are excellent credit risks. But special statutes, rules, and regulations designed to prevent graft, corruption, and favoritism are very often turned against perfectly honest tradesmen, who venture into the shark infested waters of government procurement. Municipal officials, who are employed to enforce whatever laws they know about and who have (or feel that they have) no discretion to do otherwise, often create difficulties for a tradesman hoping to do business with the city. Occasionally, long forgotten laws that have been ignored by tradesmen and by municipalities spring to life when they are discovered by a new eager beaver in a city law department.

For example, recently a court decision dredged up an obscure statute that invalidated a businessman's claim against the New York City Board of Education for goods and supplies. According to this statute, a claim was not enforceable *unless* a formal written notice of claim had been filed with the Board of Education three months after the right to make a claim arose. As a result, a tradesman, relying upon established practice and the advice of in-house lawyers generally familiar with municipal government law, was cheated out of what appeared to be a perfectly valid claim for approximately $40,000. Nor is this an isolated incident. The court decision has been applied in a series of pending cases resulting in the loss of more than $10 million by other businessmen and their lawyers who had overlooked the well-hidden statute.

For fifty years it had been assumed that contracts for the personal services of experts were not subject to the competitive bidding requirements of the New York City charter. That charter provided for competitive bidding for work, labor, and services. Exceptions were possible only by a two-thirds vote of the governing body. A company was engaged by the city's mayor to provide expert services in the reorganization of municipal functions in accordance with the existing practice. After the services were performed, the contract with the consultant was challenged. The challenge was upheld on the ground that either competitive bidding or a specific waiver of the governing body was essential to the validity of the agreement.

During a smallpox scare in the late forties, New York City's health officials used emergency orders to require pharmaceutical companies to produce vast quantities of vaccine to inoculate the entire city population. The companies rose to the occasion magnificently, devoting their resources on an emergency basis. Their efforts were applauded, but when they sent in their bills, the city's comptroller, invoking his legal authority to audit and approve payments under such emergency orders, cut them to the bone. Some of us in government, who heard the screams of the outraged contractors, worried that such an effort might never again be forthcoming in an emergency.

Guides for the Unwary

No businessman should attempt to deal with a municipality without obtaining the guidance of a lawyer skilled in that area. The courts have often held that goods and services provided and performed under a technically invalid contract with a municipality do not have to be paid for.

One further warning: municipalities, particularly large cities, are slow payers. It is usually months, sometimes many months, before you get paid for goods and services delivered to a city. So, factor a payment delay of at least three months into your price.

It is not uncommon for a city to delay monthly rental payments. A property owner in a large city reconstructed a building at considerable expense in order to rent it on a long-term lease to the city. He financed the improvements by mortgaging the property and, assuming that he was dealing with an ordinary responsible commercial tenant, he arranged for his monthly mortgage payments to come due shortly after the city rent payments would be due. But the city was a chronic late payer, and the property owner was faced with the possibility of mortgage foreclosure each month. He had to run around borrowing money at high interest to keep up his mortgage payments. Money owed by the city is not exactly money in the bank. It is there all right, but not necessarily ready money.

Do not expect to build goodwill with a city government by providing a loss leader or a free service. The city will take it, and you will get nothing for it. The kind of callous sharp practice that would ruin the reputation of a business concern is standard procedure for a municipality. For example, for many years there had been a crying need for bus stop shelters in New York City to protect citizens against the rain, snow, and wind. The city's efforts to do the job itself had failed miserably. A French organization that had developed a successful program of private construction and maintenance of these bus shelters, supported by advertising revenue in European cities, offered to do the same for New York City. The company agreed to provide and maintain the attractive bus shelters at no cost to the city and, in addition, to share the revenues derived from the operation with the city. The city had had bad experiences with a prior arrangement for street trash containers bearing advertisements, so the governing body placed the bus shelter arrangement on a trial basis for a three-year period. The city operating officials—not the governing body—assured the operator that there was no need to worry about the city giving the bus shelter deal to somebody else if it proved successful.

Well, the bus shelters were a success. They were attractive, useful, and well maintained. They proved a natural for quality advertising. Was the city grateful? You bet it was. At the end of the three-year period, although the law did not require it, it invited competitors to come in and bid for the rights. The scramble was on. The originator, which risked its resources creating something that added to the comfort of the city's people and put money in the city treasury, was outbid for a long-term contract and put out of business.

Moral: Get your arrangement buttoned down and in writing. You have no right to expect fair dealing from a municipality, only strict compliance with the forms and practices laid down by law. And watch out for contract clauses containing short—very short—periods in which to sue for claims. Six months is not uncommon. You cannot change the clauses, but you should know about them.

To Bid or Not to Bid

Doing business with the city takes three different forms: (1) contracts on sealed bids at public letting after advertising; (2) solicited unsealed bids for work supplied in a set number (usually three); and (3) open market orders. Each of these requires an explanation.

The most strict, formal, and formidable are contracts on sealed bids publicly let after advertising. This method generally applies to major city contracts for the construction of public works or purchase of vast quantities of supplies—coal, oil, gasoline—and involves the expenditure of large sums. Major construction contracts are usually bid on with the advice of engineers and cost accountants, who figure what the job is worth after a careful examination of the site and a detailed review of the bid papers and proposed contract. Lawyer specialists figure out the defects in the bid papers and the opportunities provided by the text of the proposed contract for extras above the contract price. But even with such expert assistance, major contractors occasionally make major mistakes. Recently, a consortium of contractors was engaged to construct a massive underground viaduct to supply water to New York City (consumption runs to 1,000,000,000 gallons a day). They sued the city and its Board of Water Supply for $250,000,000, claiming that they had been fooled by city engineers into drastically underbidding for the job. There were, said the contractors, hidden conditions, known only to the city, that required enormous amounts of unexpected labor and material. The consortium abandoned the work before it was half finished, totaling up a bill of $100,000,000 for out-of-pocket expenditures on labor, material, and equipment. The city counterclaimed for $369 million and defended the suit on the ground that the contractors knew perfectly well what the conditions were and made a series of costly miscalculations. In short, it was the contractors' own fault. After years of expensive litigation, the contractors settled for $23 million and in return handed over to the city special equipment valued at several million. This reduced the net amount paid to $18½ million. So, even smart businessmen, engineers, cost accountants, and lawyers are no sure protection against massive miscalculations in city construction contracts. Cost-plus contracts are not the style in city construction; they do not lend themselves to the pattern of special protective laws, which generations of municipal monkey business have brought about.

It is a common provision in municipal contract statutes that the municipality may reject all bids and re-advertise. If the city decides to award a contract it must do so *not* to the lowest bidder, mind you, but to the lowest *responsible* bidder. So even a low bid does not guarantee acceptance. A low bidder can be disqualified on any number of grounds: financial; technical; even geographical; for example, an out-of-state or even an out-of-city plant. And there is little he can do about it. To avoid being rejected in such a situation, try to arrange for advance qualification with the procurement agent in your area. Get yourself qualified as a bidder before you go through the elaborate process of pricing out a contract. Such a practice is quite common.

The forms of major municipal construction contracts are complex, and the body of laws, outside the contracts, are both elaborate and exacting. And with the involvement of federal funding, a whole new set of laws has come into play. There are affirmative action requirements for minority quotas. There are prevailing rate of wage requirements that impose the rates of pay, including such fringe benefits as pension fund contributions, guaranteed paid vacations, and required overtime in extant trade union collective bargaining agreements. There are minority enterprise requirements that obligate a general contractor to subcontract to businesses that are at least 51 percent owned and controlled by persons who are black or Spanish speaking or Aleut or Eskimo. In New York City, an executive order of Mayor La Guardia back in the 1930s and recently upheld by a federal appeals court still requires that public printing be done by a union shop and bear a union label.

Contracts for work and supplies under a fixed amount—usually ranging from $1,000 to $15,000—are often handled by open bids. The municipal purchasing agency will generally list merchants, suppliers, and contractors and inform them when work and supplies are needed or advertise in local papers or post notices. Bids are then made and accepted on the basis of price. You can get on the list by applying to the municipal procurement officer.

Small purchases—under $500 or $1,000—are standard and are often open market orders. The purchasing agent simply goes out into the market and shops for the merchandise.

Certain types of contracts for services or supplies are inappropriate for bidding and competition and therefore fall outside normal bidding requirements. Some examples are services of scientific consultants in a special field, insurance for a particular activity, and professional services of a lawyer skilled in a particular area. Finally, and more importantly, there are contracts for emergency aid. There are no cost limitations on supplies or work provided in such a situation. The smallpox vaccine referred to earlier is one example; a similar contract would be involved in cases of public calamity, storm, or major accident. In these cases, the law requires either an extraordinary majority vote of the governing body or an appropriate finding and certification of the existence of an emergency by responsible officials, and a postaudit of the bills submitted by the contractor.

Municipal contracts are commonly composed of special provisions that are based, not only on special requirements of law, but also on unique situations that took place in the dim forgotten past. And they usually incorporate by reference, that is, include elaborate bid documents by merely referring to them. Often such boiler-plate provisions have little, if anything, to do with the subject matter of the specific work, materials, or supplies involved in the contract. States generally try to achieve uniformity in the requirements for municipal contracts. However, special rules applicable to individual cities are contained in local charters and ordinances and even—as in the printing requirements of New York City —by an order of the mayor or governing body.

The important lesson to learn before signing a municipal contract is contained in the statement below. In a typical case in which a merchant was misled into a costly mistake, the court said:

> It is fundamental that those seeking to deal with a municipal corporation through its officials, must take care to learn the nature and extent of their power and authority.

Make Your Claim Promptly

Claims "upon or arising out of" contracts with New York towns cannot be made unless a verified notice of claim was presented to the town clerk within six months after the claim "shall have accrued"—that is, the contract was broken or a payment was due. In the case of a village, the time for filing a notice of claim with the village clerk is one year. But in the case of a school district or a board of education, the time for presenting a notice of claim with the governing body is a mere three months. And unlike the situation in accident claims, neither disability of the claimant or absence of prejudice to the district or board is an excuse. If you fail to comply, you are out of luck. Many a businessman has been caught without his notice of claim.

Since New York is a trend setter in protecting municipalities against claims, it should be assumed that other municipalities and school districts probably have similar laws. Merchants should be sure to protect their right to make a claim by filing a prescribed notice. Remember that local bureaucrats live by the book and are generally powerless to vary the letter of the law's requirements. Merchants, as well as accident victims, have fallen afoul of notice of claim laws.

Getting Paid

One of the problems with suing cities is that after you get a judgment you will have to wait in line to get paid. Unlike private persons or corporations, the property of a local government is ordinarily—almost always—immune to attachment, or levy of execution. In other words, you cannot get the sheriff to sell City Hall to satisfy your judgment. However, you *can* sue the city treasurer or his equivalent under another title to compel him to fork over the money owed you on a judgment.

A court order to an individual official really gets a response. Municipal officials have learned to their regret that it does not pay to disobey an order of a court. Some years ago, members of the old City of Brooklyn Board of Aldermen refused to comply with a court order directing them to issue a franchise. They were sentenced to six months in jail fo contempt of court and were allowed, as the saying goes, to swing slowly in the wind before the court granted their release after they had second thoughts and agreed to obey the court's command.

It Is Still Good Business

Yet for all this, municipalities, large and small, are an excellent source of business. They buy food for their institutions, clothing for their uniformed staff, desks, chairs, filing cabinets, carpets, brushes, brooms, cars, trucks, pins, needles, sewing machines, lamps, paint, polish, typewriters, calculators, pens, pencils, paper, paper, and more paper. The list is endless. New York City government spends vast millions a year on supplies. Its annual food bill alone is over $25,000,000. It buys annually 12,000,000 eggs, 20,000,000 quarts of milk, 10,000,000 pounds of meat, 3,500,000 pounds of fruit, and tons—yes tons—of jam and marmalade. Its yearly gasoline and oil bill comes to well over $100,000,000 for 120,000,000 gallons of heating oil and 26,000,000 gallons of gasoline. In addition, it buys 50,000 tons of coal, bringing its total energy cost to more than $400 million a year. If you know the rules and adhere strictly to them, cities, towns, and villages can be very good customers. Their credit is good and the prices at which they buy are—must be—competitive.

Bribery Is Bad Business

Do not waste your money on bribing local purchasing agents or personnel dealing with buying, selling, or leasing to or from local government. It is wrong, it is costly, it is risky. Usually, it is throwing away money for nothing. A corrupt official is the rare exception, not the rule. Generally, government purchasing agents are just doing their job. A corrupt official is dangerous; a corrupter is a fool. Both can go to prison, and, in addition, the corrupt contractor forfeits his right to get paid for any goods he has delivered and any services he has performed.

In large urban centers, there is usually a substratum of people in real estate—small-time wheelers and dealers—who are so convinced that others share their low moral standards that they commonly bribe to obtain worse deals than they could get if they were straitlaced. A career civil servant with many years of city service was put in charge of city real estate matters. He was very exacting, technical, irresponsible, and oppressive. He squeezed the last nickel out of any city deal. When he bought property for the city he badgered the seller down far below real value. When he sold city property, he demanded and got the highest possible price. It was plain torture for the seller or buyer or proposed lessor or lessee to negotiate with him. But, the supposedly slick real estate operators involved with the city official in negotiations would hand him an envelope with crisp $20 bills when the deal was finally closed. They were sure that they had bought him! Actually, as the saying goes, he was doing well by doing good. However, the silly man, who was well on the way to riches, celebrated his daughter's wedding in a gala catered affair and invited real estate, civic leaders, and top city officials—including the local commissioner of investigation. The commissioner found it somewhat bewildering that a minor functionary with a small government salary could stage such an opulent affair. The morning after the wedding, the city real estate official got a subpoena to testify in a corruption inquiry. He has not been seen since.

IN SUMMARY

1. Pay a visit to the local government procurement office, purchasing agent, general services department, or whatever agency does the buying of goods and special services and the selling and leasing of real estate.

2. Get on the list for open market orders (noncompetitive bid items) and pending real estate proposals.

3. Know whom you are dealing with. Check out his title and his area of authority.

4. Do not waste your money on bribery, it is wrong, it is risky, and it is costly.

5. On large orders and contracts that require competitive bidding, try to get prequalified, or at least some assurance that you will not be rejected as an unresponsive bidder. Obtain and study the specifications with the aid of a cost accountant and—this is really important—a lawyer who knows the prevailing rules. He can spot trouble areas in the contract, or tighten provisions that permit you to perform extra work at extra cost to the city over the bid price. Add a payment delay factor of two to six months, depending on experience, to your bid.

6. If you are outbid, check the successful bid for kinks and technical defects. If you find any, get your lawyer to protest any proposed award and sue to set aside any such award. If you succeed, you will at least get a second chance at the work or material and, if the law so provides, you may be awarded the contract by court decree.

CHAPTER IX

Zoning and
Zoning Variances

Building Regulations

Buiiding REGULATIONS, which control the construction, reconstruction, and alteration of buildings, are a common feature of life throughout the nation. Particularly in the large urban centers, the regulations are very complex and deal with minute details in regard to all aspects of structures. Hence, it is almost impossible to construct, reconstruct, or alter a building in a significant way in complete conformity with the regulations. New York City devised the first set of building laws in the United States in 1849 and has been the leader in building regulations ever since. It has pioneered the most effective safety rules for all kinds of structures, particularly places of public entertainment or assembly. Its fire laws are the most comprehensive in the nation. And, as fire tragedies and building collapses occur, New York City's codes are looked to and, in part, adopted.

The New York City Building Code is a massive document—a solid volume of law plus a volume of so-called Reference Standards. The latter are elaborate compilations of specifications for materials and equipment, which have been adopted by more than a score of government agencies and professional engineering and industrial standardization organizations. In addition there is a separate, lengthy New York City Housing Maintenance Code, a complex and detailed New York City Electrical Code, New York City Elevator Code, New York City fire laws and health laws, and a state-enacted Multiple Dwelling Law applicable only to New York City and Buffalo. There is a Multiple Residence Law applicable in the rest of New York. Federal aid for housing and urban renewal is conditional upon states' and localities' adoption of comprehensive housing codes regulating the construction, reconstruction, alteration, and maintenance of dwellings. As noted elsewhere, federal relocation requirements for persons living in the path of federally aided public highways and developments impose minimum safety and sanitary requirements for relocation dwellings. This, too, has contributed to the growth and development of building regulations all over the nation.

What to Do About the Inspector

In the face of such a massive body of statutes, ordinances, and regulations, it is not unreasonable to suspect that city building inspectors occasionally accept presents to overlook minor lapses from full compliance with building laws. There was an ingenious fellow who obtained a building permit to modernize an old brownstone in Brooklyn. On completion he needed a certificate of occupancy or approval, which would be issued only after the work was examined and certified for conformity with building laws by a city building inspector. The do-it-yourself brownstoner had no intention of giving a "present" to the inspector to encourage the issuance of a certificate of occupancy. He borrowed a black shirt and a clerical collar. "Nobody," he said, "not even a crooked inspector, would try to hit up a clergyman for a bribe." He got his certificate of approval and will never know whether it was an honorable inspector, a perfect alteration job, or the clerical collar that did it.

The complexity of building laws, the limited number of building inspectors, and the massive number of building constructions, reconstructions, and alterations in the principal cities tends to make enforcement sporadic and selective. Sometimes, inspectors simply choose easy, safe, and convenient (some say, lucrative) places to inspect. One of New York City's top elected officials, Paul O'Dwyer, once received a complaint from a lady about excessive inspection and enforcement of building laws against her house. The somewhat unusual city official went up to Harlem to see the lady. He found a neat, clean, and orderly small boarding house, operated by a hardworking widow. A building inspector had plastered it with a dozen minor violations— cracked window pane, defective radiator, missing cord on window sash, and others. The city official looked across the street and saw the dank and forbidding entrance to a rundown tenement. He realized immediately why the building inspector had been so vigilant in his enforcement against the boarding house. The inspector had no intention of venturing into the dangerous tenement house and so made up his area quota of inspections and violations in the safe territory of the widow's establishment. The hint of legal proceedings against such highly selective enforcement brought an appropriate response.

Although a certificate of occupancy is only issued after an official inspection, there is generally a time lapse between the inspection and the issuance of a certificate. Many people use that time to install facilities that are technically in violation of building codes, but involve no risk and add to the comfort of life. Often there is an unconscionable delay in the issuance of a certificate of occupancy by busy city building departments. One day the president of a large, recently completed, soft drink bottling plant was told by the company's counsel (a distinguished firm of lawyers with 75 partners and 150 associates who occupied three floors of a fancy building) that they had been unable to obtain the speedy issuance of a certificate of occupancy for the new facility. They said they could only obtain one by a lawsuit and could not estimate how much time that would take or what the result might be—not to speak of the hostility it would generate among building inspectors. The company president met a former public official, a lawyer, at a cocktail party and told him about his troubles. The former official asked him if his company was self-insured and whether the building was safe and properly constructed in all respects. The company's president assured him that the operation was perfectly safe and complained that the delay was costing his company enormous expense and loss of revenue daily. The former official then said to him, "Do you realize what would happen if you were to open and start operating? In the unlikely event that another inspection was made, you might be summoned for violating the building code and could be fined as much as fifty dollars." The company president took the hint, opened for business the next day, and lived happily ever after.[1] It would be nice to think that the company president then cancelled his retainer with the fancy law firm, whose partners were not afflicted with common sense, and took on the former and wiser government official. But that is not the way it works. He really intended to send the former official a box of cigars, but the whole matter slipped his mind in the hurly-burly of bottling lots of soft drinks and making lots of money.

---

1. The enforcement of local ordinances and laws in the major cities is, at best, spotty. New York City, as of 1979, had almost 3,000,000 ignored summonses for violations of building, peddling, and health regulations on its files. In all of these cases, there was no reasonable prospect of city enforcement.

Zoning

The single most important regulatory power of local governments is zoning, a shorthand term for the restrictions that local governments place upon land use. The second most important is the power to vary or excuse compliance with zoning regulations. This is called variance power, and will be discussed later.

Every significant local government has a zoning map and a zoning ordinance. The zoning map shows the physical areas of the various kinds of zones. The zoning ordinance describes the ways land can be used in the different classes of zones, as well as the kinds of activities permitted in such zones, the maximum height of buildings, the size of free unencumbered areas, the portion of a lot that a building may occupy, the area and width of front, back, and side portions free of construction, and so on.

Thus, zoning determines the areas in which particular uses of buildings—residential, commercial, or industrial—are permitted or prohibited. It also controls the kind of structures that may be erected in the various zones of a locality. In suburban localities, particularly, zoning power is also commonly used to exclude specific kinds of people and protect area residents from change regarded as inimical to their peace, quiet, and desired exclusivity. In urban areas, established zones are changed as neighborhoods change in the constant ebb and flow characteristic of American cities.

Zoning regulations are commonly established by elected local governing bodies. In large cities, however, zoning is adopted by the combined action of the planning board and the elected governing body. But regardless of how zoning regulations come about and who makes them, the courts have said that they are legislative in nature. This means that they have the character of a measure enacted by an elected lawmaking body. Therefore, a zoning regulation, like a statute, does not need to be proved sensible or even rational—it can be arbitrary, it can be ill-advised. It need only conform to the constitution and the statute that created the zoning agency. The result is that the only realistic chance you have to contest a zoning change is *before* it is adopted.

Variances, as we shall see, are another matter. The grant —or denial—of a zoning variance is subject to challenge in the courts if it is arbitrary, capricious, irrational, disruptive of proper planning, inconsistent with zoning schemes, or invalid on a number of other grounds.

Disagreements and contests over zoning and variances are struggles between the ins and the outs, between the merchant or builder, who wants to do what the zoning regulations say he cannot do and those who oppose what he proposes. Since this work is for the outs as well as the ins and for the merchant as well as the resident, it explains both how to obtain *and* how to prevent zoning and zoning variances.

Changing the Zoning

Local zoning agencies are much more accessible to the average citizen than legislatures. Any taxpayer can propose a change in a zone boundary or an amendment of a zoning regulation to the zoning agency. Zoning staff are planners, usually professional. They are often helpful and willing to discuss your proposals. Some zoning bodies set a particular time of year for the submission of citizen proposals. Of course, they consider proposals from other government bodies and their own staff at any time.

The official hearings for the adoption or rejection of zoning proposals are open to the public. In Sunshine law localities (see chapter XI) sessions of the planning board to discuss proposals are also open to the public.

Zoning changes, formally adopted at public sessions of local bodies, are often really determined in closed meetings.

In states that have enacted so-called sunshine laws requiring that public business be publicly conducted, zoning changes made in this way can be set aside by court review.

How to Oppose Pickle Works Zoning

Changes in zoning are opposed, proposed, or supported in much the same way that local legislation is supported or opposed, by pressure from organized citizen or special interest groups. For example, suppose the governing body of a city proposes to enlarge the boundaries of an industrial zone by adding a portion of an adjacent residential zone in order to accommodate a pickle factory, which wants to expand. Suppose you are a resident who does not want to live right next door to a pickle works. What can you do?

The first principle to recognize is that a pickle mogul, however rich and influential, has only one vote in an election of local officials—assuming that he lives in the town. The ancillary principle is that the main goal of elected officials is to be reelected. Therefore, your first step is to form a pressure group of the pickle factory despisers in your area. Do not wait until you have every last member signed up before informing the zoning body that the local residents vigorously oppose the pickle works zoning amendment. Furthermore, demand that you be informed of any and all hearings, inspections, field surveys, and proposals in regard to the zoning change. Pressure your local and state elected officials, including your congressman, for support in opposing the pickle works.

In some municipalities there is a structure for neighborhood opposition to zoning changes. In New York City it is built into the legal procedure in the form of the local community board. This board has the right of consultation, although technically, they cannot make decisions about zoning changes. However, it is not a good policy to ignore the local community board. Appear before it and make your case. If you do not appear or do not convince them, you will have an important adversary in the decision making process. In other localities, however, citizens who wish to protest a zoning change have to find or establish their own structure.

Prepare your case. Pressure without a solid factual basis is simply not enough. Get ready to establish the most cogent reasons possible for opposing a zoning change at a hearing. For example, the neighborhood opposes the pickle works because it will generate heavy traffic, disturb peace and quiet, endanger small children, create foul smells and chemical hazards in the neighborhood, overload public services and facilities, and so on. Under freedom of information laws (see chapter XI) in many states, and under general law and custom almost everywhere, the files of the zoning body are available for taxpayer inspection. Examine all applications, correspondence, diagrams, and presentations that have been submitted by the pickle people. It is entirely possible that you will discover errors, omissions, false statements, and disputable facts that can be useful as weapons in a hearing before the zoning board or, if unsuccessful there, during court review.

Select the most articulate and least flappable member of your group to make the presentation. Bombast and hysteria are seldom sufficient to carry an argument before a public body; they might help, but they also might be harmful to your cause. If you do decide that you need excitement, bring a barrel of smelly old pickles for atmosphere and arrange for a fainting lady or two.

How to Support Pickle Works Zoning

Now let us consider the other side of the matter. The pickler who wants to enlarge his plant and occupy parts of a residential zone probably does not need this book to tell him how to do it; lawyers specializing in zoning matters will advise him to conduct a campaign of persuasion before making a formal application for a zoning change. If they know their business, the lawyers will tell the pickler to leak the news that he is moving his operation out of the city. Well-placed stories to that effect will reach local newspapers and perhaps even generate editorials asking why the city is doing nothing to protect its economy and the jobs of 250 picklers.[2] The appropriate city agency will move in on the situation and try to induce the pickler to stay in the area by facilitating an appropriate zone change. The pickler, with the proper appearance of reluctance, will express a willingness to reconsider if the government will pave the way.

The "Ins" and "Outs" of Zoning

Zoning regulations are an exercise of police power—the basic authority of government to protect public health, safety, and welfare. When it goes beyond that, it is unconstitutional and an unlawful invasion of personal and property rights. In the constant struggle between the "Ins" and the "Outs," ingenuity and ingenuousness compete. To exclude everybody but the very rich, some suburban villages have adopted zoning ordinances that require a five acre minimum lot for the construction of a single family residence and totally prohibit apartment houses in the village. Occasionally, this type of zoning is successfully supported by the rationale that it preserves the ecology of the area and limits the necessity for expanded public facilities—sewers, water lines, schools, and so on. Proponents vehemently deny that it is meant to be an exclusionary tactic. Sometimes, courts see right through the

2. It is one of the mysteries of government that elected officials are far more impressed by an editorial on an inside page, which few people read, than by a news story headlined on page one, which a reader cannot avoid.

device and condemn it as unconstitutional, if it is challenged by a proposed developer. The zoning authorities then amend the ordinance to reduce the single residence requirement to four acres and permit apartment houses in the retail zone of the village. The catch is that the retail zone is fully built-up and occupied, and nobody in that zone has the slightest intention of selling out. And the developer has to go back to court.

Some zoning regulations are designed to exclude particular ethnic and religious populations. A solid WASP suburban village will adopt a zoning rule forbidding the construction of houses of worship. (The acceptable churches already there will not be affected by such an ordinance.) And when that zoning is struck down by the courts as unconstitutional discrimination, the zoning ordinance will be amended to require a vast parking lot for every new house of worship. (Again, the WASP churches will be exempt.) If that regulation is struck down by the courts, there is always the last resort of No Parking signs along the street where construction of the new house of worship is proposed. And so the battle goes on. Once the new people finally force their way in, they become the ins and the struggle to keep other ethnic or economic groups out by the old devices with new names—environmental impact, the preservation of wetlands or aridlands—goes on. And a new battle begins.

When zoning boards go too far in using their power to discriminate against classes, creeds, and colors, they can get their local taxpayers into serious trouble. Recently, as the final act in a long struggle to keep a particular racial population out of their town, the somewhat appropriately named City of Blackjack was required to pay damages of $450,000. In addition it had to rearrange its code of laws and zoning ordinances to accommodate low- and moderate-income families. In that case, the federal appeals court found that the city had adopted and fought to sustain a racially discriminatory ordinance prohibiting the construction of a multi-apartment housing project. So the court issued orders devised to achieve some measure of corrective action. Although this suit was brought by the United States Government, it could have been brought by any citizen affected, and counsel fees would have been awarded against the city. The potential of this decision can have a very inhibiting effect on exclusionary zoning all over the country.

Know the Staff Planners

There is one commonly overlooked aspect of zoning that is of major significance—the attitude and point of view of the planning agency staff. Planning staff is generally permanent; planning agency heads and elected officials are temporary. The staff very often leads, and agency heads and elected officials tend to follow staff recommendations. If you can get staff allied to your cause, your position is greatly strengthened. Conversely, if staff is opposed to your cause, your task becomes much more difficult. Never underestimate the power of the planning bureaucrat. If it is necessary to make an end run around the staff, get somebody else to do it and publicly object to the position taken by the planning agency heads.

Do not believe that flattery will get you nowhere. A member of an old New York family, who was a graduate of Groton and Princeton, was on a big city planning board. The mayor at that time was Irish and therefore considered somewhat low-class by this Ivy League gentleman. Actually, the mayor was a scholar and a poet, but hid his culture under a bushel of corn, as it were. The mayor thought the planner might be opposed to a pet project requiring planning board approval, so he cast about for some way of enlisting the aristocrat's support. One day he came across a minor monograph written by the planner on an obscure incident in city development. The mayor sent around a handwritten note telling of his delight in discovering a kindred spirit whose insightful observations had given him a most pleasant few hours in the library. He invited the planner around for a chat and charmed the poor fellow out of his mind. He never said a word about his own pet project, but by the time their talk was over, he had a staunch ally on the planning board for the remainder of his term as mayor.

If you are able to initiate and maintain a friendly relationship with planning staff, it will facilitate access—which you are entitled to in any event—to prior proposals and related matters that have come before the planning agency. Examine staff papers on such proposals, minutes of planning agency meetings, hearings, decisions, and reports on such matters. The attitudes of the decision-makers can often be discovered in talks with staff members.

Zoning Variances

A zoning law (ordinance or resolution) is a legislative act; it mandates the types of structures that can be built and activities that can be carried out in established areas or zones. In short, it covers all the details of land use. Since such laws are highly restrictive, some provision for elasticity or modification is necessary, and a body must be established to accommodate the law to the realities of social life. A zoning law might so impact upon particular land as to make it useless for any practical purpose. For this reason zoning laws are subject to variances, or exceptions, granted by a board of zoning appeals under limited authority. Generally, zoning variances can be granted only to prevent hardships. As expressed by the law, zoning variances can be made "where there are practical difficulties or unnecessary hardship in carrying out the strict letter of the zoning law, so that the spirit of that law shall be observed, the public interest preserved and substantial justice done."

A variance can be granted—or denied—only if it comes within the quoted requirements. A variance granted for reasons outside those requirements will be set aside by the court. A variance that falls within these requirements will be court ordered if denied by the variance board. As in the case of zoning, there are methods of advancing or opposing variances. The property owner must be alert if he or she wants to protect the value and convenience of the property. It is conceivable that the pickle works discussed above might be established in a residential area by means of a variance. And there is no legal stipulation that neighboring property owners must receive individual notification of an application for a variance in their neighborhood. Public notice is usually the rule; that is, formal notice posted in a government office or advertised in small print in an obscure newspaper. Usually the variance application is in the form of an appeal to rescind prior denial of a building or alteration permit. The only advice must be awareness.

Typically, variances are granted if property in a given zone cannot reasonably be used for the restricted purpose permitted in that zone and if the proposed change will not seriously affect the zone itself. For example, suppose that there is a triangular plot at the very edge of a residential zone, bordering on a commercial or light manufacture zone served by a general use highway. An application for a variance to permit the property to be used for a gas station, general service station, or a car salesroom would probably receive favorable consideration. Such property would be an unlikely site for a private dwelling, particularly since it has not been so used. The neighborhood reaction to any of these possible uses might well range from convenient to inoffensive. As a house lot, it would be hard to use or dispose of. Thus, maintaining it as an empty lot would be a hardship on the owner since the land would be subject to real property taxes.

To obtain a variance a specific procedure must be followed. Since this requires expert legal services and depends upon special circumstances, further discussion here would not be useful.

Court Review

Once a variance has been obtained or denied, swift action is necessary for court review, generally within thirty days.

In many instances, the power to grant variances is the power of life and death over businesses, and only slightly less so over homeowners. A variance permitting a gasoline and service station in a residential zone can provide a livelihood for its operator and misery for the adjacent homeowner. The stakes are high in any game involving land use. But zoning power and, more particularly, zoning variance power have often been abused in the granting and the denial of variances. For that reason, the courts have exercised a correcting power in this area more often than they have in regard to other discretionary powers of local government officials. Court review of a variance grant or denial is common and can readily be pursued. But the time limits are narrow and strictly applied. Ten day limits are not rare; thirty day limits are more common. The courts now tend to permit an expanding class of local property owners to challenge a variance grant that affects them. They include not only owners of property immediately adjacent to the site of the variance, but neighbors and even community organizations in the general area.

One interesting phenomenon of local government is that people have always mistrusted local officials. And often there is cause for mistrust. The variance power has often been abused, and in some areas no doubt still is. In New York City, the zoning variance body—the Board of Standards and Appeals—was in an advanced stage of corruption during the

1930s. Its chairman, veterinarian Doc Doyle, sold variances with almost a *prix fixe* formula. This kind of abuse has resulted in a proliferation of restrictions on municipal contracts, purchases, licenses, permits, and particularly zoning variance applications and applicants. Some of these restrictions manifest a bending over backwards attitude, which is ridiculous and self-defeating.

Consider this situation. A builder with plans to put up a lucrative subdivision applies for a zoning variance. At a meeting with the local variance officials he says, "By the way, my brother-in-law is the mayor's top assistant." That would seem to be highly irregular, wouldn't it? But in fact, under a New York statute, an applicant for such a variance or exemption is bound to do just that, under pain of going to jail if he does not. According to New York State General Municipal Law §809, "Every applicant" for such a municipal variance or exemption "shall state the name, residence and nature and extent of the interest of any . . . officer or employee of the municipality in the person making such application. For the purpose of this section an officer or employee shall be deemed to have an interest in the applicant when he, his spouse, or their brothers, sisters, parents, children, grandchildren, or the spouse of any of them is the applicant." And a person who violates the statute is "guilty of a misdemeanor."

IN SUMMARY

1. When you buy property, find out its zone and the uses permitted in that zone. You can get this information by examining the zone map and regulations.
2. Join or organize a community group to watch out for proposed zoning changes affecting your area.
3. Demand notification of proposed zoning changes from the zoning board or commission. If there is a zoning variance

or appeals board, get similar notification of variance applications affecting your area.

4. Act fast on adverse zoning changes. Obtain the rules that fix dates for challenges and appeals.

5. Prepare a case to support or oppose zoning changes or variances. Start at the grass roots level if there is reason to expect problems with the neighborhood.

6. Watch out for strict statutes of limitation for court challenge.

CHAPTER X

Licenses
and Permits

IN THE PAST, our system of free enterprise permitted anybody to pursue any profession, trade, or calling without government permit, license, or supervision. Today, however, there are few remaining businesses and no professions that can be engaged in without permit or license. Under the so-called police power—the basic authority of government to regulate people's conduct in the interest of public peace, security, health, and welfare—trades as varied as selling feathers, collecting garbage, selling fish, home improvement contracting, billiard parlors, bowling alleys, and pawnshops, are city licensed occupations. Pinball machines, which were once called bagatelle and defined as a trifling game for children, are now characterized as gambling devices and must be licensed under a set of rules appropriate for Las Vegas gaming establishments. The reason for this particular change is a story worth telling. In the late forties there was a city mayor who had a special soft spot in his heart for small candy store operators. When he discovered that some minor-league hoodlums were pushing pinball machines into candy stores, he ordered city lawyers to invent an ordinance outlawing the machines everywhere except in amusement areas under strict license requirements. The drafters decided that the only way to support such an ordinance legally was by creating a stirring statement of so-called legislative finding, a declaration included in the ordinance in which the City Council would list the conditions that had driven it to enact the provisions in order to justify the adoption of the law and make it appear to be reasonable. The ordinance drafters exceeded themselves in inventiveness in constructing the legislative finding, describing evils in pinball machines usually associated with dens of iniquity. A particularly eloquent passage described how little children squandered their lunch money and went hungry in order to play these devilish instruments. The ordinance was duly adopted, legislative finding and all, by an uncritical local council dominated by the mayor.

After a while the law fell into disuse and was commonly ignored. Then one day an eager beaver enforcement officer rediscovered it and served a summons on a neighborhood storekeeper for the operation of an unlicensed pinball machine in an unauthorized location. Instead of letting the matter blow over, the manufacturer of the game brought suit in the state supreme court to declare the anti-pinball law unconstitutional. But the court upheld the law's validity on the ground—guess what?—that little children were said to have squandered their lunch money playing the pinball machines and gone hungry to school!

And so the harboring of pinball games joined beekeeping, taxidermy, watch repairing, tree surgery, septic tank cleaning, bill collecting, lightning rod selling, and barbering as city licensed pursuits.

Even in small communities many businesses are licensed. Some communities express a curious form of xenophobia by limiting barber's licenses to persons who can prove that they have been residents of the locality for five years. Indeed, almost every significant enterprise entails some local permit or other in its day-to-day activities. The consumer has joined the humpback whale in the growing list of protected species, and this, too, has contributed to the expansion of the licensing activities of local governments.

The licensing authority of local governments is really a life and death power over the enterprises and activities involved, since they cannot operate without a license, and the power to grant one includes the power to suspend or revoke it. Requirements for local licenses and permits vary somewhat from city to city, and locality to locality. The list of occupations and activities that require a license or permit in the major cities is almost endless. It is hard to discover a trade or occupation that does not require a license by some municipality somewhere in the nation. The New York City Official Directory has a cross-indexed alphabetical tabulation of required licenses and permits—mostly municipal—which runs forty-three pages of small type. Municipalities tend to copy one another in this respect, generally adding new licensing requirements as problems arise in specific occupations—a rash of cheating by cellar waterproofing concerns, a phony going-out-of-business business, a fake check cashing service, extorting auto, radio, and television repair operators, or a fatal fire in a disco.

As a general rule, licenses and permits are granted for the asking upon payment of the appropriate fee and submission of the appropriate application form. Some licenses require pre-inspection and are subject to delay. In some cities, denial, suspension, or revocation of licenses or permits is appealable to a board of license review, and such review must be sought and refused before a court review can be obtained. Time limits for this type of administrative review vary widely, and in the event of adverse action by the licensing agency, an attorney should be retained immediately lest important rights be forfeited. Time is a critical factor because a court review might overturn the licensing agency's ruling, and the time to seek such review is limited by law. Four months is the common length of time for such review, but shorter time limits exist in particular localities. Court intervention is possible when the action of the licensing authority is arbitrary and capricious or if an abuse of power or discretion is involved.

Licensing authorities can be unfeeling at times, and it is difficult to obtain a court reversal on denial of license *applications,* particularly if the licensed enterprise has a history of unlawful activity and denial is based on moral character or criminal record. In one situation a city licensing authority refused to grant a locksmith license to an applicant because he had been convicted of forgery thirty years before. He had to appeal to a high court after a lower court rejection to finally win a decision in his favor. Another applicant who sought permission to work on the docks as a longshoreman was not as fortunate. A licensing commission denied the permit because the applicant had an old criminal record. The decision was upheld by a three to two vote of an appeals court in particularly unhappy circumstances, moving a dissenting judge to unusual eloquence:

His last criminal offense was over 15 years ago. Actually, he worked on the docks, as a cooper, until 1960, without incident; and had worked as a longshoreman until 1958, having started at the age of 17 years. It was the only way of life he knew and loved. Said he: "Well, I have been down here most of my life. I was contented with the work. It's a good income for my family. It's my whole life since I have been a kid."

It thus seems particularly poignant to me, and a social and economic waste, to deny this able-bodied veteran an opportunity now to do hard labor because of some misdeeds done in the long ago under the stress of temptations about which we know not. He petitions us now not to work in Tiffany's, nor at Fort Knox, nor as a cashier in a bank. He begs the privilege of wielding a bale hook on the open piers, in the cold of winter and the heat of summer, in order to put bread on the family table. I vote to give him a chance.

We have before us a family man, 45 years of age, whose only work skills are attuned to the waterfront. For 10 years he has been forced to scrounge around, unsuccessfully, for odd jobs as a janitor, trucker, bartender, to support an ailing wife and a child, getting by only by help from veterans welfare. He has stayed straight and clean for 15 years. He comes supported by attestations by professionals in social work, by the family physician, and by neighbors. And there is nothing in this record to controvert these representations that the applicant is completely rehabilitated. Society cannot possibly suffer from an extension of mercy by permitting this man to do hard work, on the unrefuted evidence of this rehabilitation. Quite the reverse.

City licensing authorities are often prejudiced by moral qualities and criminal records and commonly deny licenses on that basis. As Profesor Walter Gelhorn of Columbia University once noted, in some localities the only occupation open to a once-convicted felon is burglary. In Georgia cities you must pass a Wassermann test for syphilis before you can get a license to work as a photographer.

Licensing officials naturally tend to rely upon police reports for arrest and conviction records. This kind of information is particularly vital for licenses that involve contact with households. Occasionally, licenses have been denied because a partner in a licensed business had a police record that turned out to be erroneous. Data banks are not always perfect. A recorded crime might turn out to be a defectively recorded parking ticket or some other minor violation that would not even qualify as a misdemeanor. A recorded dismissal from a job actually might have been a voluntary resignation. Names and dates can be mixed up, and memories confused. What is remembered as or thought to be a dishonorable military discharge may turn out to be nothing of the sort. So, if your license application is rejected, insist on knowing why *specifically*. You might be able to demonstrate that the decision is wrong. It has happened. And make your correction on the record in writing to provide a basis for court review if it should become necessary. Fortunately, in New York State a recent statute forbids the denial of a license to a former criminal unless he was convicted of a crime bearing directly upon the licensed activity, such as, for example, a persistent sex offender who wants to be licensed in an activity requiring daytime visits to private homes.

Courts are not loath to overrule the revocation or suspension of a license or permit, particularly when such action means a loss of livelihood. And the general rule is that such a suspension or revocation—as distinguished generally from an application—requires a full trial type hearing, including the right to be represented by counsel. At such a hearing, use every possible piece of evidence in your favor because it is likely that the record you compile will be the only document a court can look at when reviewing the administrative action taken. If you are denied a license, demand a hearing whether or not you are entitled to one under the law. And collect every scrap of material that might help and put it on the record. If your morals or background are the claimed basis of a denial, get written testimonials from priests, rabbis, former employers, and teachers. If your application for a license is delayed for a long time, do not hesitate to complain and badger whoever is delaying it. The screaming child and the squeaking wheel get attention. So, squeak and, if necessary, scream. And if all else fails, get a lawyer and sue. You might even have a 1983 suit.

There is, of course, another side to licensing—the real justification for it—protection for the general public. A licensed business does not want the licensing agency to receive complaints about its practices. If you feel cheated by a licensed lightning rod installer or cellar waterproofer or television repairer, the threat of complaint to the license department will make an impression. In fact, an actual written complaint will be far more effective—and cheaper—than a law suit against the cheating merchant. And if you fail to get reasonably prompt action from the license bureau, do not hesitate to complain to the mayor, the chairman of the board of supervisors, or the county executive. You might be pleasantly surprised at the fast action. Of course, heads of local government vary in this regard. Some might never see your letter, some might just send it on to the file-and-forget clerk. Fiorello H. La Guardia, a no-nonsense New York City mayor, paid close attention to complaints mailed to his office. He tried to read them all and when he did, he acted in his usual no-nonsense manner. La Guardia sent complaint letters to the appropriate officials and attached different colored slips depending on the urgency of the matter. A red slip attached to a complaint letter gave commissioners the jitters and got fast, very fast, action.[1]

It is probable that there is a license requirement for the following activities in your locality:

1. aircraft landing places
2. ambulance service
3. amusement devices and arcades
4. auctioneers
5. bakers
6. beauty parlors
7. billiard rooms

---

1. There was an instance of this, unrelated to licenses but worth noting if only because it has not been recorded anywhere else. There was a young lawyer assigned to a pretty lowly job in a minor city agency. Somebody wrote a letter to the mayor accusing the young man of carrying on with a stenographer in the office. One morning, he got an envelope from the mayor's office. Inside was the accusing letter with the terrifying red slip, endorsed with the signature initials "F.H.L.G." and the message "CUT IT OUT." The lawyer, now old and gray, told me that it almost drove him to a life of celibacy.

8. bowling alleys
9. cabarets
10. cabs
11. catering
12. circuses
13. dance halls
14. day care centers
15. dogs
16. dry cleaning
17. employment agents
18. dumps
19. fireworks
20. funeral homes
21. gasoline service stations
22. hospitals
23. home improvement contractors
24. locksmiths
25. movie theaters
26. milk and milk products
27. newsstands
28. parking lots
29. peddlers
30. plumbers
31. refuse removal
32. security guards
33. septic tanks
34. side shows
35. sidewalk cafes
36. stables
37. street fairs
38. swimming pools
39. taxis
40. theaters
41. undertakers

Licensing Bureaus

In large urban centers there is usually a separate department of licenses, and, in addition, government agencies dealing with health and fire prevention have their own license and permit sections.

In small communities, the city clerk is the functionary in charge of receiving license applications. He, in turn, submits them to the local governing body.

It is not possible to set forth a useful tabulation of the local government licensing agencies; they are obviously numerous and varied. To find out where to apply for a license and when licenses are needed, check local city and county directories or the local government attorney or clerk.

Getting a License

The initial process for obtaining a license is the same all over, submission of an application form supplied by the local licensing agency. Almost every license application must be accompanied by a fee fixed by law. (Often, the fee involved has stimulated local governments to require particular licenses.) Usually, the process is short and simple. It tends to get more complicated when public health and safety is directly involved.

A license cannot be denied except for a valid reason; the denial cannot be arbitrary or capricious, but must be for reasons relating to the fitness of the applicant to properly conduct the activity for which the license is sought. If you are refused a license, you are entitled to know why. If you are already in an occupation where a new license requirement is enacted, you are entitled to a license, and it cannot be denied unless there is reasonable cause. If it is denied, you have the right to a hearing and you can bring a lawyer, question witnesses, and produce evidence. An occupational license cannot be cancelled or suspended unless there is good and sufficient cause based upon evidence at a hearing. The licensee is entitled to appear at that hearing with a lawyer, examine and cross-examine witnesses, and produce evidence.

CHAPTER XI

The Right
to Find Out

IT IS A little-known fact that municipal governments in the United States are the most open and visible governments in the world; almost all their proceedings and records are available for public scrutiny. Every state has a freedom of information law and an open meetings law of one kind or another. Some are more liberal than others, but all provide a substantial measure of openness in local (and state) government.

In obtaining relief from municipal mischief and enforcing claims against municipalities, one of the citizens' most useful allies is the new body of laws guaranteeing access to government information—the sunshine laws and the freedom of information acts. The so-called sunshine laws require that public business be publicly transacted in full view of the public. The freedom of information acts ensure that the papers, documents, and records of public agencies are available for public scrutiny. Public records have always been subject to inspection in a limited way, but the definition of a *public record* was very narrow. Under the new freedom of information acts, almost every piece of paper in a public office is available on demand. And you need not divulge your purpose in making such a demand.

It is very important to know that you have rights, and it is equally important to get the facts that will help you establish those rights. For example, the federal freedom of information statute, applicable only to federal offices, is widely used by industries seeking information on their competitors' operations and practices and by lawyers looking for material in a variety of situations. Federal agencies require detailed reports on all sorts of matters, and this kind of information can be very useful in formulating a case against the government or in obtaining background material on a given subject. Very little is sacred or secret to most government agencies.

Searching for Information

Suppose you have been in a collision with a city truck. You will want to know when the truck was inspected and you will want to see the inspection report. You will want to see the accident report filed by the driver of the truck and any report made by his superiors. You will want to know what other accidents the driver and/or the truck were involved in. You will want to know if any disciplinary proceeding has ever been brought against the truck driver. Suppose you have been assaulted or robbed in a city park, hospital, or other public facility. You will want to know if other similar instances have occurred, what reports have been made, and what security recommendations have been proposed and ignored. Suppose you suspect that contract bids have been rigged or that conflicts of interest exist that invalidate a competitor's bid on a city contract. The best place to look is in the city's own files. All this, and much more, is available in any state that has a freedom of information act, usually known as F.O.I. Municipal record keeping is absurdly detailed and often quite slovenly, but it is a mine of material that can be useful to your cause. Generally, local government personnel fill out forms without considering how such forms will be used and write reports and memoranda that can later prove most embarrassing to the municipality.

New York City has had a liberal public access provision in its charter for more than fifty years—long before freedom of information acts became widespread. Some years ago, a special referee was appointed by the court to determine how much tax a large utility had to pay the city. He showed his proposed report, which favored the city, to certain city officials and told them he would not sign and file it until he received his fee of $50,000. The city officials wrote a memorandum to the city comptroller explaining the situation and urging the issuance of a check for the referee. The special referee got his check, and the city got the report, duly signed and filed. The utility, in preparation for a legal protest of the report—a protest thought to be pretty hopeless—got the city file on the subject and discovered the memorandum among the rest of the papers. The consequences were very disagreeable for the city and very embarrassing for the writer of the memorandum.

More recently, a construction contractor who instituted a massive lawsuit against a city received some unexpected help from an examination of the city's files. His attorney discovered a detailed memorandum from a city lawyer that concluded that the contractor would be likely to recover damages in the suit because city employees had supplied inadequate information at the time of bidding.

A franchise to construct bus shelters on New York City sidewalks became the subject of competitive bidding when a temporary franchise expired. (See page 114 for further details.) The holder of the temporary franchise, who had invested a great deal in his idea, began a massive document search of the city's files. He came up with enough material to stir up a great deal of mischief, generate an official investigation, and hold up approval of a contract to the successful bidder.

The usefulness of the F.O.I. laws can hardly be overstated, and the many ways they can be applied are a challenge to your imagination. All information pertaining to sidewalk and roadway defects—origin, condition, and any prior notices that were received—are recorded somewhere in municipal files. Their usefulness in an accident case, whether or not city negligence is involved, can be really significant, and the record is there for the asking. Telephone logs, diary notes, time sheets, and visitor records can provide all kinds of helpful information to use in ways only proscribed by the limits of your imagination.

Similarly, the worksheets and notes of real property assessors can be inspected and copied. Their surveys and notes can make your condemnation case. These documents can establish unlawful discrimination—deliberate overassessment of some properties and underassessment of others for purposes of taxation or city acquisition. You also have the right to examine building inspection and permit records, public contract files, disbursement and payroll records, and lists of the names and addresses of property owners and tenants in a proposed site for a highway project or other public facility. You can find out how much the city paid out in condemnation awards and as compensation for relocation and moving expenses. You can obtain access to police blotters to seek evidence of unlawfully selective prosecution for building code violations. If, with all this material available, you are taken advantage of, it is not the fault of the law—assuming you live in a state with a liberal F.O.I. law. Even if you live in an area where access to municipal documents is limited to public records, you can still demand and receive a considerable amount of information.

Freedom of information requests can produce all kinds of

useful material that you can use to prevent or promote zoning changes or applications for zoning variances or building permits. You can also obtain valuable information to help support or oppose applications for licenses or permits to engage in controlled occupations or activities. And you do not have to limit yourself to municipal government files. The federal F.O.I. Act can also be used. There are very few activities that are not subject to federal regulation in one way or another. Significant F.O.I. demands are tabulated each week in a nonofficial publication called *The National Law Journal*. The listed items are good examples of the kind of information you can demand.

Federal agency files offer an almost limitless source of information that can be used to deal with municipalities as a litigant or citizen. The National Highway Traffic Safety Administration has files on traffic patterns and the conditions of all kinds of highways, automobiles, and trucks. This material can be extremely helpful in accident cases or contract claims. The Federal Environment Protection Administration has reports, surveys, and analyses on all kinds of products and areas. This kind of information could become the basis for opposing—or supporting—the establishment of various kinds of commercial or industrial enterprises in zoning or zoning variance proceedings. The Federal Consumer Protection Safety Commission maintains a massive file of esoteric information on injuries and damages caused by a wide variety of products commonly used by individual consumers and municipalities. You can reach into the files of the FBI and find out if your local police or another local agency has been spying on you. And if they have, you might have a 1983 suit. (See chapter IV.)

In short, there's no limit to the fun—profitable fun—you can have with the F.O.I. laws.

How to Look at the Records

New York's Freedom of Information Law, which is modeled on the federal F.O.I. Act, is typical of the trend in states throughout the country. Here is how it works:

All records in public offices are accessible on demand, with the following exceptions:

1. records that cause an unwarranted invasion of a person's privacy
2. records that impair present or imminent contract or collective bargaining negotiations
3. records that reveal trade secrets
4. records that interfere with law enforcement or judicial proceedings
5. records that deprive a person of a fair trial
6. records that reveal the identity of a confidential informer in a criminal investigation or any criminal investigation techniques that are not routine.

The name, address, title, and salary of every public officer and employee must be made readily available for inspection and copying in each public office. Public offices are also required to maintain a current subject list of all types of records in its files.

Each public agency must designate a records access officer, whose name and location must be posted or otherwise publicized, to keep record lists current and available for inspection and copying.

For example, suppose you were assaulted on a subway train platform. It certainly would be useful to know if similar instances had taken place in that station. Such information might indicate neglect by the transit agency.

There is no special request form required by law. Simply make your request in writing and reasonably describe what you are looking for. A written demand can be as simple as this:

> To: City Transit System,
> Pursuant to the freedom of information law, you are hereby directed to provide me with copies of the following records of your agency: all inspections and reports of crime incidents, arrests and complaints in regard to the Fourteenth Street Station during the period January to September, 1979.
> Please inform me as to the charges and the date when I may receive these records.
>
> > Joe Nudge
> > 60 Pine Street
> > New York, N.Y. 10007

Records must be made available within five days after the request is made. If your request is denied, you are entitled to know the reason. You can appeal a denial to the head of the agency or governing body involved and appeal any further denial to the courts in an expedited proceeding. Copying fees may not exceed the actual cost of photocopying.

The courts have vigorously enforced the F.O.I. law in New York and in other states with similar statutes. Unfortunately, unlike the federal statute, counsel fees for successfully obtaining a court order for agency denied material is not provided in the New York State law. Perhaps the state legislature was scared off by the federal F.O.I. case in which the government agreed to pay an interim fee of $200,000 with much more to come.

Let the Sunshine In

The so-called Sunshine Law requires that municipal board and council meetings for the purpose of conducting public business be open to the public. There is only one exception.

In limited circumstances, a closed session—commonly called an executive session—can be held if it is authorized by a majority vote of the board at a public meeting. The purpose of such an executive session must be stipulated at the public meeting as well. Furthermore, no final action can be taken by an executive session, and no decisions can be reached. Closed sessions can only deal with strictly limited matters:

1. matters that might imperil public safety if disclosed
2. matters that reveal the identity of an undercover law enforcement person or an informer
3. proposed employment or disciplinary proceedings or medical or credit matters
4. criminal investigations which, if disclosed, might affect the outcome
5. discussion of pending or current litigation, labor negotiations, or real property deals

The only other exemption from Sunshine Law requirements is the deliberation of regular courts, most administrative courts, and administrative boards like a board of zoning appeals or a tax commission.

If a municipal board acts in private or on the basis of deliberations held in private or otherwise violates the open meeting law, its action may be set aside by a court. And under the Sunshine Law, the court is also empowered to award counsel fees to the protesting citizen.

Before sunshine laws were enacted, public bodies, boards, and councils commonly reached their decisions in private and merely announced them in public, even if they were required to take action at a public meeting. Some did not even bother to announce their decisions publicly; they simply issued the decisions and had them formally filed in a public office.

The sunshine laws changed all that. No more back room deals. No more smoke-filled rooms. So far, attempts to lessen the effects of open meeting laws have been rejected by the courts. Some public bodies have tried to disguise meetings by calling them planning sessions, agenda discussions, informal conversations, or work sessions. Such devices have met with judicial disapproval. Whatever its name, if it is a meeting for the transaction of public business, it falls within the province of sunshine laws. There is very little that an official board of commission can do without letting the public know what is going on.

If you suspect that a municipal board is likely to conduct a cozy private session in the home of one of its members to deal with a matter that you are interested in, you can act in either of the following ways. You can knock on the door and demand admittance. You can also bring along your own crowd of allies for the discomfiting and intimidating effect of their presence. You might actually be invited in. Or, you can keep quiet and wait to see how the matter is finally resolved in a later public session. If it is favorable, you will not have to take any further action. If it is not, sue to have the decision set aside on the ground that the public announcement was merely a rubber stamp of the determination made in an unlawful *executive* session. Demand counsel fees as well. This kind of action is quite common. Local boards and councils of various kinds are still not accustomed to Sunshine Law requirements. The courts are setting aside decisions made in private and announced in public almost every day. An entire body of rent control guideline regulations adopted by a New York City board was set aside by the court on the ground that it was actually worked out at private meetings of board members that were neither announced to the press nor open to the public. The court remanded the entire matter to the board for complete—and public—consideration.

CHAPTER XII

People Power

Starting a Revolution

LOCAL GOVERNMENT OFFICIALS and bureaucrats only *seem* implacable. Actually, they are vulnerable and can easily be swayed by people without influence. The trick is to *appear* influential. First, create an organization and invent an impressive name for it, preferably one that lends itself to an acronym: Democratic Action Group (DAG); Political Action Center (PAC); New Affiliated Citizens (NAC); or Progressive Era Politics (PEP). The Committee of a Thousand or Ten Thousand is another good title. However, very large numbers may cause a few raised eyebrows and do not have the aura of exclusiveness that marks a group like The Four Hundred, for example. So choose your name carefully and make sure that it conveys the impression that you are a branch of a significant organization. Once you have settled on a name, visit a printer and design a letterhead. Have it professionally typed and offset. Proper stationery can be a great help in creating a good impression.

Next, get members. You will be surprised by the number of people who love to join organizations and involve themselves in causes. Before you know it, you will be a community leader! Now, pick a cause: street repairs, new sewers, garbage collection, better police protection, or lower taxes. If you would rather focus on broader issues, choose a larger cause, call for government restructuring or the cancellation of salary increases voted by elected officials for elected officials. Remember, people generally do not like their elected officials to get paid at all.

Now you are ready to move. Issue press releases. Denounce government policies and officials. Under United States Supreme Court rulings, you do not even have to be too zealous in checking your facts; it is almost impossible to be successfully sued for libel by a public official!

Retirees, an ever growing section of our population, may be particularly interested in this kind of government participation. They, more than any other part of the population, have the time, the maturity, and the skill to play a useful and interesting role in practical politics and the molding of municipal policy.

What Can Be Done

Never underestimate the power of the people. Even a small group of determined citizens can change important decisions made by major public officials. Robert Moses, the great master builder of New York City, was regarded as unopposable in his days of power. Yet, when he proposed that a major limited access highway be cut through Brooklyn Heights—a superb eighteenth- and nineteenth-century area overlooking the East River—the Heights lovers banded together to oppose the plan. However, unlike other such groups that simply mount opposition, they had enough sense to offer an alternative that Moses was quick to embrace. The result was a three-level highway, which was cantilevered off the Heights cliffside and was topped with a pedestrian promenade overlooking the river and offering a magnificent view of the New York Harbor and the downtown skyscrapers of the financial district.

Initiating a Popular Referendum

Initiative and referendum provisions were introduced into American local government in the 1900s by good-government groups as a progressive measure to reform corrupt local governments and deal with corrupt politicians. Many states have similar provisions, but we are primarily concerned with the local provisions here.

The Proposition 13 syndrome that began in California has alerted people to these provisions in municipal charters, statutes, and state constitutions. Although these provisions are now being used as a tax revolt device, they were designed to serve a wider purpose. Citizen groups can get closer to the root of local government and deal with the actual causes of inefficiency. For example, these provisions can be used to require that zoning changes be submitted to popular vote.

Defining Terms

Initiative is the right of citizens to initiate laws, to act as a legislative body. It is direct law-making by the people. In effect, a group of citizens can propose that the people themselves enact a law. Initiative can operate in either of two ways. A citizen or a group of citizens can draw up a petition that presents the proposed law itself, or the petition can call for the formation of a citizens' commission to prepare a new body of laws to govern the locality or to change the form of the locality's government.

Referendum is the method by which the people directly express their approval or disapproval of a proposed law or proposal to create a citizens' law-amending commission. It appears on an election ballot as a proposition and is voted on at a regular election or a special election.

Initiative and referendum laws are common throughout the country. They make it remarkably easy to completely restructure local governments. For example, in New York City, with a population of more than 7,700,000, a referendum to establish and choose members for a charter revision commission can be initiated by the petition of 45,000 voters. This amounts to less than ⅗ of 1 percent of the people who would be directly affected. An amendment of a local law to limit real estate taxes can be initiated by a petition of 30,000 voters, followed by an additional petition of 15,000. Such local law will then go on the ballot for a referendum.

In New York State, the governing bodies of cities, counties, towns, and even villages exercise the power to adopt local laws and ordinances subject to community scrutiny and a considerable degree of community control. For example, basic laws of the locality—such as the nature of the governing body, the way in which members are elected, their terms of office, and the assignment of their powers—can only come into being if they are approved by popular vote. Certain other essential powers can be legislated by the local governing bodies, for example, public notice requirements, public bidding and contract requirements, auditing methods, and sale of real property. These powers are only subject to the people petitioning to put them on the ballot at referendum. County and city people in New York can petition to enact local laws and not only change their county or city charter, but create and name charter revision commissions to completely alter the form and character of their government. And the procedures for all this are really quite reasonable.

Recently, the elected officials of New York City altered the city charter to give themselves whopping salary increases, including a $20,000 a year raise for the mayor and substantial raises for the city comptroller and for the president of the city council. The council also voted itself nice fat raises. There was some editorial support for the raises. But as noted in an earlier chapter, editorials do not necessarily—perhaps rarely—reflect the attitude of the people.

Acting under a New York statute, a group of objectors started to collect signatures on a petition that would require a public vote on the matter. However, the method they chose required 150,000 valid signatures to get the question on the ballot. And since the objectors were amateurs, and petition signature gathering is a rather technical procedure, it was estimated that no fewer than 300,000 signers would actually be necessary to survive the legal attempt to discover technical defects in the petitions. The result was that there simply was not enough time to generate enthusiasm, and the method failed to accumulate enough signatures to put the matter on the ballot.

Here is the actual form of petition used in the effort to stop the pay increases. It is a useful model.

IMPORTANT: YOU CANNOT WITNESS YOUR OWN SIGNATURE, SIGN ANOTHER REGISTERED VOTER'S PETITION. SIGNATURES AND ADDRESSES MUST BE LEGIBLE. DO NOT FILL IN SHEET NO. WITNESS MUST INITIAL ANY CHANGES OR CORRECTIONS. WE WILL FILL IN A.D. AND E.D. (COUNTIES: FOR MANHATTAN ENTER N.Y., FOR BROOKLYN ENTER KINGS, AND FOR STATEN ISLAND ENTER RICHMOND. BRONX AND QUEENS ARE PROPER.) RETURN PETITIONS AS SOON AS COMPLETED TO OUR TOWN NEWSPAPER, 500 E. 82 ST., N.Y.C. 10028.

PETITION FOR A REFERENDUM ON THE NEW YORK CITY LOCAL LAW OF 1979 RAISING THE COMPENSATION OF THE MAYOR, COUNCIL MEMBERS AND OTHER CITY OFFICIALS

We, the undersigned qualified electors of the City of New York, pursuant to section 24 of the Municipal Home Rule Law, hereby protest against the local law of the City of New York introduced on June 28, 1979, passed by the City Council as Int. No. 713 and entitled "A LOCAL LAW No. 37 to amend the New York City charter in relation to the compensation of the mayor, the president of the city council, council members, borough presidents and the comptroller." As required by such section of the Municipal Home Rule Law, we demand that such local law be submitted to referendum at the next general election and not take effect unless approved by the affirmative vote of a majority of the qualified electors of the City of New York voting on a proposition for the approval of such local law at such election.

Each of the undersigned petitioners protesting such local law and demanding a referendum thereon subscribes as follows:

I, the undersigned, do hereby state that I am a duly registered elector of the City of New York, qualified to vote in such city, and that my place of residence from which I am registered is truly stated opposite my signature hereto.

Date	Name of Signer	Residence	Assembly District	Election District	County
1. /79					
2.					
3.					
4.					
5. , etc.					

STATEMENT OF WITNESS

I, _____, state: I am a duly
        (name of witness)
qualified and registered voter of the State of New York. I now reside at _____ which
                    (fill in residence address)
is in the _____ election district of the _____ Assembly
            (fill in no.)   (fill in no.)
district in the County of _____ in the City
                        (fill in name of county)
of New York.

Each of the individuals whose names are subscribed to this petition sheet, containing _____ signatures, subscribed the same in my presence on the date above indicated and identified himself to be the individual who signed this sheet.

I understand that this sheet will be accepted for all purposes as the equivalent of an affidavit and, if it contains a material false statement, shall subject me to the same penalties as if I had been duly sworn.

_____

Signature of Witness

_____   Sheet Number _____

Dated

Actually the objectors would have been better off using a different method to achieve a similar result. Under the same law, only 30,000 petition signatures are necessary to propose an initiative-adopted local law that could amend the city charter to cancel out the salary raises and forbid any future raises without the approval of the people at a referendum.

Obviously, it is much easier to get 30,000 valid signatures than five times that many.

To complete the process, an additional 15,000 signatures would be necessary two months later. But if the first campaign was successful, the momentum could very well carry over and make the second round much easier.

The petitions themselves would contain the proposed charter amendment and its title and text could be made very attractive to voters. For example:

WE THE UNDERSIGNED QUALIFIED ELECTORS OF THE CITY OF NEW YORK HEREBY PETITION TO AMEND THE NEW YORK CITY CHARTER AS FOLLOWS:

A LOCAL LAW TO REPEAL LOCAL LAW NUMBER 37 OF NINETEEN HUNDRED SEVENTY-NINE AND CANCEL THE MAYOR'S $20,000 RAISE, THE COMPTROLLER'S AND COUNCIL PRESIDENT'S $15,000 RAISE AND COUNCIL MEMBERS' $10,000 RAISE, AND REQUIRE THAT SUCH RAISES BE SUBJECT TO POPULAR REFERENDUM IN THE FUTURE.

Section 1. Sections four, twenty-five, and ninety of the New York City Charter are hereby amended to read as follows:

§4. ELECTION; TERM; SALARY. The mayor shall be elected at the general election in the year nineteen hundred sixty-five and every four years thereafter. He shall hold office for a term of four years commencing on the first day of January after his election. The salary of the mayor shall be [Eighty] *sixty* thousand dollars a year.

§25. SALARIES. a. The salary of the president of the council shall be [Seventy] *fifty* thousand dollars a year. b. The salary of each council member shall be [Thirty] *twenty* thousand dollars a year.

§90. ELECTION: TERMS; SALARY. The comptroller shall be elected by the electors of the city at the same time and for the same term as in this charter prescribed for the mayor. His salary shall be [Seventy] *fifty* thousand dollars a year.

Section 2. Section thirty-nine of such Charter shall be hereby amended by adding thereto a new item to be item number nineteen to read as follows:

19. increases the salary of an elected official.

Section 3. This local law shall take effect immediately upon its adoption.

EXPLANATION: matter in *italics* is new; matter in brackets is old law to be omitted.

The election district number and the assembly district number (or ward number and town, as required in the particular state or locality) and the other material, as above, is filled in by the persons organizing the petition drive. In large cities, print-outs of voters and their identified locations are usually provided by election officials.

There is an odd fact about the initiative and referendum requirements for locally enacted laws in New York. It is more difficult to *reduce* the salary of an elected official in New York City than it is to *increase* it. The city official cannot reduce the salary of an elected official all by itself. Any such local law it passes does not take effect until it is approved by the vote of the citizenry at the next general election. But, a local law increasing such a salary, as we have seen, takes effect unless at least 150,000 voters sign valid petitions to put it on the ballot at the next general election. History reveals the reason for this strange fact. The initiative and referendum provisions of the New York City charter, which serve as a model for many local governments, came about during Fiorello La Guardia's administration. As a reform mayor, he was in constant battle with a Tammany Hall dominated city council during his time in office. It was felt, not without reason, that unless there was a curb on its power, the city council would cut La Guardia's pay down to one dollar a year, just to show who was in control of New York. Times have changed, but the law has not.

There is no better way to discover how local government works than to become a member of a charter revision commission. From that vantage point you can look into government agencies and operations, and you will find that there are no mysterious forces at work and that genius is no more prevalent in government than it is in commerce, finance, or industry. Occasionally initiative and referendum laws are used for faddist, trivial, or comic reasons. Last year California had an anti-smoking proposition on the ballot. In the mid-nineteenth century the New York legislature received a petition calling for a referendum to establish a convention to amend the state constitution to give executive and legislative powers to the directors of the New York Central Railroad. The legislature duly complied, and the referendum lost by only 6,000 votes.

Initiative petitions must be carefully drawn, and signatures must be properly obtained in technical compliance with the law. You can look up old petitions in the files of the city clerk or the election officials. They will provide an appropriate pattern for your campaign. The mystique of the political process is really not hard to learn. If you spend a single afternoon in a district office of a political campaign, you can obtain all the knowledge you need.

California municipalities are probably the most initiative and referendum addicted of all. In the 1978 general election, for example, there were ten "County Questions" and seven "City Questions" on the ballot voted by the People of the County and City of Los Angeles. The issues were quite varied. One proposed that certain activities performed by government employees be contracted out to private concerns. Another proposed to remove administrative positions in the sheriff's, assessor's and district attorney's offices from civil service, and to accord the same treatment to county supervisor's deputies. There was a proposal to completely restructure the county government and a proposal to forbid certain county employees from performing work in an area detached from Los Angeles county. There were *advisory* proposals for the provision of rail transit from the Los Angeles airport to the railway station and a bus and carpool *guideway* from the airport to the Convention Center. A city proposition called for a change in the way board of education members were elected. Another proposed a limit on city expenditures for the 1984 Olympic games. All this was in addition to eight elaborate statewide referenda propositions ranging from initiative statutes regulating cigarette smoking to the employment of homosexuals in public schools to the punishment for murder. Also included were initiative amendments regarding the accreditation and licensing of chiropractic schools; a $500,000,000 veterans' farm and home aid bond issue; constitutional amendments about selling surplus coastal property; and property tax reform dealing with reconstruction after a disaster.

The bewildered Los Angeles voter received a series of five

detailed pamphlets explaining all the propositions, discussing the pros and cons of each, and analyzing the detailed text.

After going through all this material one is left with a feeling of deep sympathy for the Los Angeles voter, who must look forward to Election Day with considerable apprehension.

Correcting Municipal Mischief

The ordinary citizen has vast unused powers to discover, prevent, and correct government waste, inefficiency, and corruption. He can act as a municipal bounty hunter and receive rewards beyond the thrill of achievement.

City charters often contain provisions to encourage taxpayer involvement in keeping local government officials on the straight and narrow path. For example, since 1897 the New York City charter has provided that "any five citizens who are taxpayers" can petition a state supreme court justice to conduct "a summary inquiry into any alleged violation or neglect of duty in relation to the property, government or affairs of the City." Although there have certainly been instances of violation or neglect of duty by New York City officials in the past eighty-plus years, the charter provision has never been used successfully. The few attempts to employ it were said to duplicate existing investigations and were rejected by the courts.

Charters and statutes in other states and cities have related provisions, but they too are often neglected and only occasionally brought to life. For example, in the 1960s the San Francisco tax assessor was the object of a grand jury investigation and he was indicted and later convicted of taking bribes to underassess property for tax purposes. Four taxpayers sued to cancel the incorrect assessments, make new assessments, and recover the appropriate taxes. The court granted judgment as demanded and ordered the municipality to pay the expenses incurred by the taxpayers out of the moneys it had collected plus "sums fixed in accordance with a schedule of the property tax revenues collected (20 percent of the first $1 million, 10 percent of the second, and 5 percent of the third)" as counsel fees.

A few years ago, in a suburban town adjacent to New York City, a taxpayer, who was also a lawyer, succeeded in recovering a large sum paid by a local government for an electric generating installation purchased in deliberate violation of competitive bidding laws. The court not only compelled the contractor to give back most of the money, but the local government got to keep the generator. The lawyer-taxpayer was awarded a substantial fee for his efforts.

In 1977 the California courts awarded a lawyer's fee of $170,000 to an environmental group for successfully opposing a general plan for Los Angeles that did not conform to environmental laws. The same year the California courts awarded Public Advocates Inc. and Western Common Law and Poverty—two voluntary legal services enterprises—$400,000 each for successfully challenging the state method for financing public education.

Fees have been allowed a non-lawyer who brought suit against municipal officials by himself.

POSTSCRIPT

THE ACTIVITIES OF local government are constantly expanding. From the simple provision of police and fire protection, primary and secondary school education, street sweeping, water supply, and sewage disposal, municipal government has grown into a multi-purpose, multi-service entity. It touches our lives in countless ways. There is hardly an activity or enterprise that some local government does not engage in or have some involvement in. And, as cities, towns, counties, villages, and the host of local special governments take on a wider variety of functions, their bureaucratic structures proliferate and their impact on us increases.

Municipal governments take more and more of our resources, both directly and through the grants of federal and state revenues that are provided by our tax dollars. They impinge upon our daily lives, and control our work and our play to a significant degree. The forces of local government have the capacity to be benign or malign, and our influence over these forces is limited. However, influence of any kind is impossible without an understanding of the structure of local government and a knowledge of our rights.

In the beginning of the book, I said that you have got to know that you have rights before you can assert them, and, when you know what those rights are, you have got to know how to protect them. I have tried to take the mystery out of local government and provide you with the means to protect yourself against its mischief and enjoy its benefits.

Too many of us shrug our shoulders in resignation and say, "You can't fight city hall." But indeed, you *can* fight and often *beat* city hall—if you know how. And that is what this book is really all about.

APPENDIX

APPENDIX A: Notice of Claim Form

New York City's Notice of Claim is very similar to the form used by many other municipalities. Before filing such a notice, study this sample carefully. The form has been divided into two parts. FILL OUT only the information requested in the part that appears directly below. Include your attorney's name if you are being represented by legal counsel.

CLAIM AGAINST THE CITY OF NEW YORK
PERSONAL INJURIES

This Claim must be filed in duplicate either in person or by registered mail within 90 days from the date of damage at the Office of the Comptroller, Municipal Building, Room 608, Centre and Chambers Street, Manhattan 10007.

To The Comptroller of The City of New York: I herewith present my claim against The City of New York

TYPE or PRINT INFORMATION

PERSONAL INFORMATION

NAME OF CLAIMANT	LAST	FIRST		AGE	DATE OF BIRTH MONTH/DAY/YEAR	IF MARRIED, SPOUSE'S FIRST NAME
ADDRESS	NUMBER & STREET		CITY (BOROUGH)	STATE	ZIP	HOME PHONE—

ACCIDENT INFORMATION

DATE OF ACCIDENT MONTH/ DAY /YEAR	EXACT LOCATION OF ACCIDENT _____
TIME ☐ AM ☐ PM	
DESCRIBE HOW ACCIDENT HAPPENED	

The remainder of the form appears below. DO NOT FILL OUT any of this information. A municipality is *not* entitled to this information, and it can be used against you in a court of law.

WAS THERE A WITNESS TO ACCIDENT? ☐ YES ☐ NO	IF YES, GIVE NAME AND ADDRESS OF WITNESS TO ACCIDENT		LAST	FIRST	
ADDRESS OF WITNESS	NUMBER & STREET		CITY (BOROUGH)	STATE	ZIP
WERE POLICE PRESENT AT ACCIDENT? ☐ YES ☐ NO	NAME OF POLICE OFFICER	LAST	FIRST	BADGE #	PRECINCT#

MEDICAL INFORMATION

WHERE WAS FIRST MEDICAL TREATMENT RECEIVED?				DATE OF FIRST TREATMENT MONTH/ DAY/ YEAR
WAS CLAIMANT TAKEN TO HOSPITAL BY AMBULANCE? ☐ YES ☐ NO	WAS CLAIMANT TREATED IN EMERGENCY ROOM? ☐ YES ☐ NO	CLAIMANT ADMITTED TO HOSPITAL FROM: _____ TO: _____		
NAME OF DOCTOR TREATING INJURY		ADDRESS OF DOCTOR	NUMBER & STREET	CITY(BOROUGH) STATE ZIP
DESCRIBE YOUR INJURY IN DETAIL				

EMPLOYMENT INFORMATION

CLAIMANT'S OCCUPATION AT TIME OF ACCIDENT	☐ EMPLOYED ☐ UNEMPLOYED	☐ HOUSEWIFE ☐ RETIRED	IF EMPLOYED: WEEKLY SALARY $		NUMBER OF WORKING DAYS LOST IF ANY
EMPLOYER'S NAME					AMOUNT OF PAY LOST, IF ANY $
EMPLOYER'S ADDRESS	NUMBER & STREET	CITY (BOROUGH)	STATE	ZIP	PHONE

DOCTORS AND HOSPITAL EXPENSES

HOSPITAL BILLS, IF ANY $		ARE BILLS SUBMITTED WITH CLAIM? ☐ YES ☐ NO	DOCTOR BILLS, IF ANY $		ARE BILLS SUBMITTED WITH CLAIM? ☐ YES ☐ NO
LIST ALL OTHER EXPENSES CAUSED BY ACCIDENT					

FILL IN THIS SECTION IF ACCIDENT INVOLVED N.Y.C. OWNED VEHICLE

WAS CLAIMANT THE OWNER OF VEHICLE INVOLVED IN COLLISION? ☐ YES ☐ NO, IF NO:	OWNER'S NAME	LAST	FIRST	
OWNER'S ADDRESS	NUMBER & STREET CITY (BOROUGH) STATE ZIP	WAS CLAIMANT A PASSENGER IN VEHICLE ☐ YES ☐ NO, IF NO:	WAS CLAIMANT THE DRIVER OF VEHICLE ☐ YES ☐ NO

N.Y.C. VEHICLE AND DRIVER INFORMATION

NAME OF N.Y.C. DRIVER	LAST	FIRST	N.Y.C. LICENSE PLATE NUMBER
EMPLOYED BY	DEPARTMENT	TOTAL AMOUNT CLAIMED AS DAMAGES $ FOR THIS ACCIDENT _____	

APPENDIX B: Tax Assessment Reduction Form for Homeowners

GROUP No. ☐

BOROUGH ___ **BLOCK** ___ **LOT** ___ 19___/19___

TAX COMMISSION OF THE CITY OF NEW YORK
APPLICATION FOR CORRECTION OF TENTATIVE ASSESSED VALUATION FOR NON RENT PRODUCING PROPERTIES

PROPERTY INFORMATION

BLOCK ☐ LOT ☐

BOROUGH (Check one only)

Manhattan (1) ☐   Bronx (2) ☐   Brooklyn (3) ☐   Queens (4) ☐   Staten Island (5) ☐

PROPERTY ADDRESS

Number ___   Street ___

APPLICANT

Name ___   Phone ___

RELATION OF APPLICANT TO PROPERTY (Check one only)

Owner ☐   Lessee ☐   Vendee ☐   Mortgagee ☐   Receiver ☐   Other ☐   Specify ___

APPLICANT ADDRESS (As Above ☐ or)

Number ___   Street ___   Zip ___

City, Town or Village ___   State ___

ATTORNEY OR AGENT

Name ___   Phone ___ - ___

ATTORNEY OR AGENT ADDRESS (As Above ☐ or)

Number ___   Street ___   Zip ___

City, Town or Village ___   State ___

NOTICE OF DETERMINATION (Check one only)

Send to (a) Applicant ☐   (b) Attorney/Agent ☐

TENTATIVE ASSESSED VALUATION   19 8 ___ /19 8 ___

Land $ ___   Total $ ___

CLAIMED FULL (MARKET VALUE)
ON JANUARY 25 OF THIS YEAR $ ___

IS A PERSONAL HEARING REQUESTED   YES ☐   NO ☐

Grounds for Objection (Applicant must check one or more): Illegality ☐   Overvaluation ☐   Inequality ☐

If this application alleges illegality, specify the grounds of the alleged illegality ___

If this application alleges over-valuation, state the extent of such over-valuation ___

If this application alleges inequality, specify the instances in which such inequality exists and the extent thereof ___

1. Property has been:
    (a) Sold within 2 years prior to January 25th of this year ☐
    (b) Is under a contract to sell ☐

    SALE DATE/   AMOUNT
    CONTRACT DATE

    [   ] $ [   ]
    Month   Year

                        GRANTOR

    [   ]

2. Financing information (Complete if sold or refinanced within 2 years prior to January 25th of this year)
    (a) Property has been sold   ☐
    (b) Property has been re-financed   ☐
    (c) Loans for construction have been made ☐

MORT-GAGE NUMBER	PRINCIPAL	ANNUAL INTEREST RATE	AMORTI-ZATION PERIOD	TERM	DATE MORTGAGE ASSUMED Month Year
[ ]	$ [ ]	[ ] . [ ]	[ ]	[ ]	[ ]
[ ]	$ [ ]	[ ] . [ ]	[ ]	[ ]	[ ]
[ ]	$ [ ]	[ ] . [ ]	[ ]	[ ]	[ ]

3. Building information (Complete if constructed or altered within 2 years prior to January 25th of this year)
    (a) A new building has been constructed   ☐
    (b) An existing building has been altered ☐

    YEAR OF   COST OF
    CONSTRUCTION/ALTERATION   CONSTRUCTION/ALTERATION
    [1 9   ] $ [   ]

4. Last year settled   19 [   ] /19 [   ]

    AMOUNT OF SETTLEMENT   TAX COMMISSION   TRI-DEPARTMENT BOARD   PRE-TRIAL
    $ [   ]   ☐   ☐   ☐

5. Appeal Status of Court Cases:
    (a) Appeal pending   Yes ☐   No ☐

    (b) If no appeal is pending, time to appeal has expired   Yes ☐   No ☐

6. Other facts submitted to support full value   Yes ☐   No ☐
    Facts submitted:
                                                                    Date
                                              Yes   No   Month   Year
    (a) Bankruptcy   ☐   ☐   [   ]   [   ]

    (b) Foreclosure   ☐   ☐   [   ]   [   ]

    (c) Other (specify)_____   ☐   ☐   [   ]   [   ]

If application is not signed by the aggrieved party (or in the case of an aggrieved corporation, by an officer thereof), it must be accompanied by a Power of Attorney.

State and City of New York, County of_____ , ss.

_____ , being duly sworn, says under penalty of perjury, that he is the applicant or

the_____ of the applicant, that the statements contained in this application (including the attached

sheet(s) consisting of_____ pages) are true to his personal knowledge, that applicant claims to be aggrieved by the aforesaid assessed valuation and makes application to the Tax Commission to have the same reviewed and corrected and asks that the assessed valuation for the year indicated on the face of this application be fixed at $_____ .

Sworn to before me this_____

day of_____ 19_____

_____
                Signature of applicant or representative

_____
Person authorized to administer oath

APPENDIX C: Tax Assessment Reduction Form for Commercial Dwellings

GROUP No. [ ]

BOROUGH _____ BLOCK _____ LOT _____ 19 ___ /19 ___

TAX COMMISSION OF THE CITY OF NEW YORK
APPLICATION FOR CORRECTION OF TENTATIVE ASSESSED VALUATION
FOR RENT PRODUCING PROPERTIES ASSESSED FOR LESS THAN 1 MILLION DOLLARS

PROPERTY INFORMATION

BLOCK [ ]   LOT [ ]

BOROUGH (Check one only)

Manhattan (1) ☐   Bronx (2) ☐   Brooklyn (3) ☐   Queens (4) ☐   Staten Island (5) ☐

PROPERTY ADDRESS
Number [ ]   Street [ ]

APPLICANT

Name [ ]   Phone [ ] - [ ]

RELATION OF APPLICANT TO PROPERTY (Check one only)

Owner ☐   Lessee ☐   Vendee ☐   Mortgagee ☐   Receiver ☐   Other ☐   Specify ____

APPLICANT ADDRESS (As Above ☐ or)
Number [ ]   Street [ ]   Zip [ ]

City, Town or Village [ ]   State [ ]

ATTORNEY OR AGENT

Name [ ]   Phone [ ] - [ ]

ATTORNEY OR AGENT ADDRESS (As Above ☐ or)
Number [ ]   Street [ ]   Zip [ ]

City, Town or Village [ ]   State [ ]

NOTICE OF DETERMINATION (Check one only)
Send to (a) Applicant ☐   (b) Attorney/Agent ☐

TENTATIVE ASSESSED VALUATION   19 8 ___ /19 8 ___

Land $ [ ]   Total $ [ ]

CLAIMED FULL (MARKET VALUE)
ON JANUARY 25 OF THIS YEAR $ [ ]

IS A PERSONAL HEARING REQUESTED   YES ☐   NO ☐

Grounds for Objection (Applicant must check one or more): Illegality ☐   Overvaluation ☐   Inequality ☐

If this application alleges illegality, specify the grounds of the alleged illegality _____

If this application alleges over-valuation, state the extent of such over-valuation _____

If this application alleges inequality, specify the instances in which such inequality exists and the extent thereof _____

APPENDIX C: (*Continued*)

1. Property has been:
   (a) Sold within 2 years prior to January 25th of this year ☐
   (b) Is under a contract to sell ☐

SALE DATE/
CONTRACT DATE   AMOUNT

[ ] $ [ ]
Month Year

GRANTOR
[ ]

2. Financing information (Complete if sold or refinanced within 2 years prior to January 25th of this year)
   (a) Property has been sold ☐
   (b) Property has been re-financed ☐
   (c) Loans for construction have been made ☐

MORT-GAGE NUM-BER	PRINCIPAL	ANNUAL INTEREST RATE	AMORTI-ZATION PERIOD	TERM	DATE MORTGAGE ASSUMED Month Year
[ ] $ [ ]		[ ] . [ ]	[ ]	[ ]	[ ]
[ ] $ [ ]		[ ] . [ ]	[ ]	[ ]	[ ]
[ ] $ [ ]		[ ] . [ ]	[ ]	[ ]	[ ]

3. Building information (Complete if constructed or altered within 2 years prior to January 25th of this year)
   (a) A new building has been constructed ☐
   (b) An existing building has been altered ☐

YEAR OF
CONSTRUCTION/ALTERATION   COST OF
CONSTRUCTION/ALTERATION

1 9 [ ] $ [ ]

4. Last year settled 19 [ ] /19 [ ]

AMOUNT OF SETTLEMENT   TAX COMMISSION   TRI-DEPARTMENT BOARD   PRE-TRIAL
$ [ ]   ☐   ☐   ☐

5. Appeal Status of Court Cases:
   (a) Appeal pending   Yes ☐ No ☐
   (b) If no appeal is pending, time to appeal has expired Yes ☐ No ☐

6. Other facts submitted to support full value   Yes ☐ No ☐
   Facts submitted:

	Yes	No	Date Month	Year
(a) Bankruptcy	☐	☐	☐	☐
(b) Foreclosure	☐	☐	☐	☐
(c) Other (specify)_____	☐	☐	☐	☐

SCHEDULE OF INCOME AND EXPENSES FROM _____ 19____ to _____ 19____

Check one ☐ Cash basis   ☐ Accrual basis

I. INCOME INFORMATION

A. USE	CHECK	B. RENTABLE AREA	C. NUMBER OF UNITS/SPACES	D. RENTS 1. RENTAL INCOME	E. INCOME FROM ESCALATION 1. OPERATING EXPENSE	2. TAX ESCALATION	F. TOTAL
(a) Apartments				$	$	$	$
(b) Stores				$	$	$	$
(c) Offices				$	$	$	$
(d) Lofts				$	$	$	$
(e) Warehousing/Industrial				$	$	$	$
(f) Garages/Parking				$	$	$	$
(g) Storage				$	$	$	$
(h) Other				$	$	$	$
(i) TOTAL				$	$	$	$

G. INCOME FROM PERCENTAGE LEASES $ [ ]

H. COMMON AREA CHARGES $ [ ]

I. SALES OF UTILITIES/SERVICES
1. Electricity   2. Heating   3. Air Conditioning   4. Other Services
[ ]$ [ ]   [ ]$ [ ]   [ ]$ [ ]   [ ]$ [ ]   TOTAL [ ]$ [ ]

J. OTHER INCOME
1. Laundromat   2. Vending Machines   3. Miscellaneous
[ ]$ [ ]   [ ]$ [ ]   [ ]$ [ ]   TOTAL [ ]$ [ ]

K. TOTAL GROSS INCOME $ [ ]

APPENDIX C: (Continued)

II. EXPENSE INFORMATION

A. MANAGEMENT/ADMINISTRATION

1. Management Expenses	2. Professional Fees and Expenses	3. Advertising and Pro-rated Leasing Expenses	4. Membership Fees
$	$	$	$

5. Insurance Pro-rated	6. Other Management Expenses		TOTAL
$	$		$

B. LABOR AND RELATED COSTS

1. Wages	2. Benefits	3. Value of Employee Accommodation	TOTAL
$	$	$	$

C. UTILITIES

1. Electricity	2. Water and Sewer	3. Heating Type	4. Heating Costs
$	$	Gas □ Oil □ Electric □ Steam □ Coal □ Solar □	$

5. Air Conditioning	6. Cooking Fuel Residential Tenants	7. Rubbish Removal	8. Telephone	TOTAL
$	$	$	$	$

D. SUPPLIES/PARTS

1. Office	2. Cleaning	3. Operating Supplies/Spare Parts	4. Other Supplies	TOTAL
$	$	$	$	$

E. MAINTENANCE/REPAIRS

1. Interior Areas	2. Interior Mechanical (a) Elevator	(b) Plumbing	(c) Electrical	(d) Heating/Ventilation
$	$	$	$	$

3. Cleaning Contract	4. Exterior Areas	5. Exterior Mechanical	6. Other Maintenance	TOTAL
$	$	$	$	$

F. DECORATING

1. Halls/Common Areas	2. Tenant Areas	3. Exterior	TOTAL
$	$	$	$

G. TAXES, PERMITS AND FEES

1. Real Estate Taxes	2. Payroll Taxes	3. Permits, Licenses and Fees	TOTAL
$	$	$	$

H. MISCELLANEOUS COSTS

1. Alterations to Tenants Areas	2. Other Expenses		TOTAL
$	$		$

I. TOTAL EXPENSES $

III. NET INCOME
(Total Gross Income less Total Expenses)

NET INCOME $

IV. ADDITIONAL INFORMATION REQUIRED

A. OWNER OCCUPIED SPACE

1. Net Square Footage Occupied OR	2. Percent Occupied	3. Claimed Current Rental Value
		$

B. VACANCY AND COLLECTION LOSS

1. Percent Vacant Apartment Units	2. Percent of Commercial Area Vacant	3. Amount of Loss
		$

C. LAND OR GROUND RENT	D. BUILDING RENT
$	$

INSTRUCTIONS

1. Tax Commission Rules of Practice and Procedure

This application is governed by the Amended Rules of Practice and Procedure of the Tax Commission, a copy of which may be obtained at the Borough Offices listed below:

These rules prescribe, among other things:

(a) the types of evidence which must be submitted in support of particular factual claims (Rule X (b));

(b) that the application must be filled out fully and legibly in typescript or in permanent ink (Rule XIII); and

(c) An offer of reduction must be accepted by the applicant on the proper form within ten (10) days after the offer is made (Rule XIV (f)).

Failure to abide by these rules may result in confirmation of the tentative assessment.

2. Time and Place of Filing Application

The application must be filed between February 1st and March 15th in the Borough Office of the Real Property Assessment Bureau in which the property is located: Manhattan: Municipal Building, Centre & Chambers Streets, New York, N.Y. 10007; The Bronx: Bergen Building, 1932 Arthur Avenue, Bronx, N.Y. 10457; Brooklyn: Municipal Building, Joralemon & Court Streets, Brooklyn, N.Y. 11201; Queens: 90-27 Sutphin Boulevard, Jamaica, N.Y. 11435; Richmond: 350 St. Marks Place, Staten Island, N.Y. 10301.

3. Income and Expense Information

Commissioners are not authorized to offer a reduction of the tentative assessed valuation in the absence of an income and expense statement except where the applicant has not owned and operated the property for a major portion of the preceding year and is without knowledge of the income and expenses of the operation. In this case applicant shall state such facts under oath in lieu of the income and expense statement. (New York City Charter §163 and Administrative Code §E 17-16.1)

The income and expense statement is divided into four parts: Part I Income; Part II Expenses; Part III Net Income; and Part IV Additional Information Required. A split rectangular box is provided for all items within the first Part sections I and J; Part II sections A through H and Part IV sections C and D.

Use the larger portion of each box to record the amounts. Use the smaller portion to indicate that expenses have been grouped.

EXAMPLE A

SALES OF UTILITIES AND SERVICES (Item J of Part I)

1. Electricity	2. Heating	3. Air Conditioning
1 \$5,000	1 \$	1 \$

Explanation: The number 1 in the smaller boxes shows that sales of electricity and air conditioning have been grouped.

EXAMPLE B

SALES OF UTILITIES AND SERVICES (Item J of Part I)

1. Electricity	2. Heating	3. Air Conditioning
1 \$5,000	1	1

Explanation: The number 1 in the smaller boxes shows that now 3 sales items have been grouped in the electricity amount.

NOTE: The aggregate amount should always be placed in the first applicable box (see the examples below). If there is more than one aggregated item, they should be numbered in sequence as shown in the next example.

EXAMPLE C

SALES OF UTILITIES AND SERVICES (Item J of Part I)

1. Electricity	2. Heating	3. Air Conditioning
1 \$5,000	1	1

MANAGEMENT/ADMINISTRATION

1. Management Expenses	2. Professional Fees
2 \$1,000	2

DECORATING (Item F of Part II)

1. Halls/Common Area	2. Tenant Areas	3. Exterior
3 \$2,000		3

TAXES, PERMITS AND FEES (Item G of Part II)

1. Real Estate Taxes	2. Payroll Taxes	3. Permits, Licenses & Fees
	4 \$500	4

NOTE: Aggregate items can be grouped across Major Item Numbers; for example, if Management fees, Professional fees and Wages are grouped, this would be shown as follows:

EXAMPLE D

MANAGEMENT/ADMINISTRATION (Item A of Part II)

1. Management Expenses	2. Professional Fees
2 \$1,000	2

LABOR AND RELATED COSTS (Item B of Part II)

1. Wages	2. Benefits	3. Value of Employee Accommodation
2		

Likewise if Supplies were grouped with the Decorating of Hall/Common Areas and Decorating of the Exterior this would be shown as follows:

EXAMPLE E

SUPPLIES/PARTS (Item D of Part II)

1. Office	2. Cleaning	3. Operating Supplies/Spare Parts
		3 \$2,000

DECORATING (Item F of Part II)

1. Halls/Common Areas	2. Tenant Areas	3. Exterior
3		3

INDEX